THE ULTIMATE GUIDE TO
KNIFE THROWING

THE ULTIMATE GUIDE TO
KNIFE THROWING

MASTER THE SPORT OF KNIFE AND TOMAHAWK THROWING

BOBBY BRANTON

FOREWORD BY STEPHEN MCEVOY

Skyhorse Publishing

Skyhorse Publishing books may be purchased in bulk at special discounts for sales promotion, corporate gifts, fund-raising, or educational purposes. Special editions can also be created to specifications. For details, contact the Special Sales Department, Skyhorse Publishing, 307 West 36th Street, 11th Floor, New York, NY 10018 or info@skyhorsepublishing.com.

Skyhorse® and Skyhorse Publishing® are registered trademarks of Skyhorse Publishing, Inc.®, a Delaware corporation.

Visit our website at www.skyhorsepublishing.com.

10 9 8 7 6 5 4 3

Library of Congress Cataloging-in-Publication Data is available on file.

Cover design by Rich Rossiter
Front cover photographs by Terrill Hoffman (top left image), Tony Carico (top middle and top right), and Daniel Stevens (bottom)

Print ISBN: 978-1-63220-530-8
Ebook ISBN: 978-1-63220-912-2

Printed in China

TABLE OF CONTENTS

ACKNOWLEDGMENTS

I first would like to dedicate this book to my Mom who always believed in me and stood by me my whole life. To my loving wife, Brenda—I am very grateful to have such a great wife who has supported me and all of my wild entrepreneurial endeavors over the past thirty-three years that we have been together. Some worked, some didn't, but she was by my side the whole time telling me to keep trying and that she knew I could do whatever I set my mind to. She has been my biggest supporter, my greatest fan, and my best friend from day one.

I also would like to thank my good friends, Stephen D. McEvoy and Mr. and Mrs. Kenneth Pierce (Che Che and Nancy). And a special thanks to Ralph Thorn and Tim Valentine for their insight and contributions that helped make this book a reality. Stephen has stood by me from day one when I asked if I could bring back the AKTA (American Knife Throwers Alliance). Stephen's friendship means the world to me.

Che Che and Nancy have been friends to Brenda and I for many years and they have been huge supporters of the AKTA. Brenda and I love you both.

To my friend Larry Brahms, who has never given up on me—who has helped me go over Hollywood contracts, given me business advice, given me life advice, and who checked on me every night while this insecure author and knifemaker made his first trip out of the country to work a film in Mexico City. Larry, you are the best friend ever.

I also want to thank all of the friends and customers who have supported Branton Knives and The American Knife Throwers Alliance. The greatest compliment that a craftsman can receive is to have hard working people pull their hard earned money out of their pockets to buy my knives. For this, I am truly humbled.

—Bobby Branton

Branton in motion

ABOUT THE AUTHOR

As a young man growing up in rural South Carolina, Bobby Branton developed a passion for knives that has stayed with him throughout his adult life. In his younger years, knives were tools used for skinning game, filleting fish, and throwing as a means of entertainment. Then in 1983, edged weapons took a different perspective in Branton's life when he discovered some custom knives in a local shop. He was amazed at the beauty and craftsmanship of these handcrafted blades and started his own collection. His interest grew so readily that he read every book he could locate on the subject and decided to try his hand at knife making.

After constant reading, research, and collecting of knives, Branton reconstructed his shop in order to create these treasured handcrafted knives. Through his research he discovered one common factor, a man named George Herron. He was a master craftsman who had a seven-year wait for his custom knives. Mr. Herron soon befriended Branton and a close bond formed between the two craftsman. Branton purchased knives from him while gaining much advice and valuable pointers.

Branton makes his working knives by the "Stock Removal Method" and by hand forging various metals. His style has obviously been influenced by George Herron and Walter Brend along with forging techniques from well-known Master Bladesmith, James Crowell.

Branton has become an expert knifemaker and was awarded his "Journeyman Bladesmith" stamp at the 1992 Blade Show in Atlanta,

Georgia by the American Bladesmith Society. Branton met legendary blademaker Harry K. McEvoy in 1987. McEvoy taught Branton the fine art of handcrafting throwing knives; he also helped design Branton's first series of throwing knives. Branton has since designed several models of throwing knives that have been used to win major knife-throwing competitions across the country.

Another turning point in his career was when Branton met knife-throwing legends Paul LaCross and Kenneth Pierce (Che Che Whitecloud). LaCross was billed as "The World's Foremost Knife, Axe, and Tomahawk Thrower". It was Paul who taught and motivated Branton to put together a throwing exhibition which he performs throughout the Southeast.

LaCross retired in 1990 due to health reasons and passed away in 1992. In 1996 with the help of Stephen McEvoy, Kenneth Pierce and his wife Nancy, and a few close friends, Branton was instrumental in reorganizing the American Knife Throwers Alliance and held what has been arguably the first knife- and tomahawk-throwing-only contest in over twenty years.

He has assisted numerous individuals in starting knife-throwing contests around the world. During some contests Kenneth Pierce still comes down to visit Branton and his wife Brenda once a year to assist in preparations for the American Knife Throwers Alliance National Championships and is one of the club's biggest supporters.

Branton has been promoting the art of knife throwing by giving seminars on the subject since 1996. Also, in 1996 Branton was awarded the South Carolina State Folk Heritage Award for the work in bladesmithing and for preserving the traditions of South Carolina. While promoting knife throwing to the general public, Branton has taught thousands of Boy Scouts and even a number of Army Rangers as well as few celebrities the fine art of knife throwing.

Over the years Branton's knives have been featured in most of the annual publications about knives and he and his work have been featured in other publications such as *Knife World*, *Blade* magazine, *Tactical Knives*, *Knives Illustrated*, and *South Carolina Wildlife*.

Branton has handcrafted knives for such greats as Paul Lacross; Che Che Whitecloud, who is billed as "The Fastest Knife Thrower in the World"; knife-throwing great Larry Cisewski; former governor of South Carolina, Carroll Campbell; and the former governor of Texas, George W. Bush, who has gone on to be president of the United States.

Branton's knives are sold and exhibited all over the world with avid consumers in England, Germany, France, Israel, Australia, Japan, and Canada. One of Branton's throwing knives now resides in the world famous Randall knife museum in Orlando, Florida.

Over the years, Branton has been a consultant to a number of production companies who sought out his expertise in knife throwing for shows such as *Guinness World Records*, *Fear Factor*, *That's Incredible!*, and magazines such as *Maxim* and *Men's Health*. Branton has authored four articles on the subject for *Blade* magazine and one article for the 5th annual *Levine's Guide to Knives*.

In 2004, Branton was hired by a production company to be a technical advisor and to train actress Salma Hayek for a role in a new movie *Bandidas* to be released in January 2006. Branton was flown to Los Angeles to train Ms. Hayek for the role of a bank robber who happens to be an expert with knives. After the training in Los Angeles, Branton was flown to the movie set in Mexico City to further train Ms. Hayek and to act as a technical advisor during filming.

A couple of weeks later after leaving Mexico City, Branton was flown to Durango, Mexico, where he performed the actual throwing on location for the more difficult throwing scenes. Branton also designed and crafted some very special throwing knives for Ms. Hayek and actor Sam Shepard to use in the film.

In addition to making and throwing knives, Branton has become an "aficionado" of the western arts of whip cracking and traditional archery. As a result of the deaths of Paul LaCross and Harry K. McEvoy, a great loss is felt in the brotherhood of knife throwing and traditional archery. Therefore, Branton vows to preserve and promote the dying arts of the old West. During his career, Branton has become involved in promoting his craft and keeping tradition alive.

IMAGE 1

Bobby Branton's South Carolina Folk Hertiage Award

IMAGE: 2

Bobby Branton's AKTA membership card.

Bobby Branton

FOREWORD

Bobby Branton, the author of the work you are about to read, is a modest and unassuming man, honest and humble. Quite a contrast for someone so accomplished in the endeavors described in this book. In addition to the knife and tomahawk seminars he gives at the annual Blade Show, Bobby has instructed film stars in the correct practice and style of knife throwing for movie roles; has instructed knife and tomahawk throwing for US Army Rangers at their annual Best Ranger event; consulted on several formats of social media in the art and practice of knife throwing; and actively demonstrated correct throwing form and technique in myriad other circumstances. He is also the National Director of the American Knife Throwers Alliance (AKTA), a national organization for the perpetuation of knife and tomahawk throwing as a recreational sport.

Aside from his many professional knife-throwing talents, Bobby is also a superb custom knife maker, crafting excellent throwing knives for over twenty-five years, as well as a variety of hunting, combat, and tactical folding knives. As you progress through the manuscript you will see that he is eminently qualified to instruct you in all the nuances of the knife-throwing genre. Not since the books by Harry McEvoy has there been as complete a comprehensive guide as you are about to read.

What more could be said? Bobby Branton is a true professional in every definition of the word. You could not take better direction from anyone more accomplished. Enjoy the book!

Stephen McEvoy
President
Tru-Balance Knife Co.
Grand Rapids, Michigan

THE ULTIMATE GUIDE TO
KNIFE THROWING

CHAPTER 1

HISTORY

PIONEERS OF KNIFE THROWING

As a young boy growing up next to my uncle's meat processing plant, I have been exposed to knives nearly all of my life. I hung around and eventually worked in that meat processing plant during grade school and most of my high school years. I was fascinated with almost any type of knife and one of my earliest memories of knife throwing was watching actor Ed Ames on the *Johnny Carson Show*. Ames's claim to fame at the time was for his role as Mingo, a Cherokee tribesman on the TV series *Daniel Boone*. During the interview, Ames claimed that he could hit a target from across the room, and Carson asked Ames if he could demonstrate this skill. Ames agreed, and a wood panel with a chalk outline of a cowboy was brought on to the stage. Ames proceeded to throw the tomahawk, which hit the "cowboy" square in the groin with the handle pointing upward. This led to a very long burst of laughter from the audience. Whenever I am traveling around the country doing seminars or demonstrations, without fail, someone will always ask me if I saw that clip on television.

As I grew older, I began to research and seek out the knife-throwing acts and learn about the people who threw knives for a living. I was in awe of their skills and would try to emulate these skills in private, but without the proper equipment, I had little to no success.

Knife-throwing performers are known to have performed in Europe and America in the nineteenth century with recorded uses of the term "impalement" to describe this type of act as early as the late 1800s.

The growth of the impalement arts was greatly aided by the way that the circus developed in the nineteenth and early twentieth centuries, and in particular by American influences. Buffalo Bill's performances in Europe in 1887 resulted in a wave of popularity for wild west shows and the "western arts" they involved, including knife throwing, archery, whip cracking, and sharpshooting. In the circus world, the success of large-scale tented touring shows pioneered in America led to the introduction of more acts of skill and daring as well as the inclusion of sideshows, in which impalement acts sometimes were featured. Among the most significant events were the Barnum & Bailey circus tours of Europe from 1897 to 1902, which made a huge impact on European circus owners and led them to adopt similar formats. As well as providing a friendly stage where impalement acts could rely on finding an audience, the circus was a competitive environment in which shows and performers sought to outdo each other and so created incentives to develop new stunts. Moving targets were an innovation used by European artists in the 1930s. A notable example is the wheel of death, which is believed to have been introduced into the United States in 1938 by the Gibsons, from Germany.

PROFESSIONAL KNIFE THROWERS OF THE PAST

THE GIBSONS

Joe and Hannah Gibson were originally from Germany, but later performed in the United States and have been credited with bringing the heel of death stunt to America. They featured in Ringling Brothers and Barnum & Bailey shows at Madison Square Garden in 1938.

Frank Dean

Frank Dean was born in California, and after completing his high school education toured the country with various circuses, wild west shows, and vaudeville units.

During the 1929 season with the Al G. Barnes circus, he did his knife-throwing act in addition to trick riding and fancy roping numbers. Here he worked with two other noted knife throwers, Frank Chicarello and Bennie Pete.

In 1935, his novelty knife-throwing act was a sensational feature of the entertainment program presented at the Grand Yokohama Exposition in Japan.

Upon his return in 1935, he started the manufacture of throwing knives. This came about from the many requests for knives from people witnessing his knife-throwing act. His 10-inch knives gained popularity, and continued requests for information on knife throwing prompted him to write his first book on knife throwing.

His experience as a soldier in World War II added to his knowledge of the use of a knife in combat.

Frank Dean passed away in 1985.

George "Skeeter" Vaughan (aka Grey Otter)

George Vaughan was a Cherokee who served in the US Army in the second world war and worked at various times as a lumberjack, Hollywood stunt man, and impalement artist. He made numerous national television appearances including *Truth or Consequences*, *Thrill Seekers*, a minor role in *Magnum, P.I.*, and performances on *Circus of the Stars* in 1977 with actress Ann Turkel as his target girl and again in 1979 with Charlene Tilton braving the knives. He died in 1989.

George "Skeeter" Vaughan

Sylvester and Barbara Braun

Sylvester and Barbara Braun, who were good friends of knife thrower and trick roper Frank Dean, were billed as "The Wizards of the West". Their show involved trick riding, whips, ropes, throwing knives and hatchets. They were married in 1952 and were both circus performers. The two of them were working in the Clyde Beatty Railroad Circus when they first met. Barbara and Sylvester were ropers and riders. They learned most of their knife-throwing skills from fellow circus performer, Bennie Pete, who was the circus knife thrower. Sylvester used to throw ten knives very fast around the spinning wheel to which his wife Barbara would be strapped to, using the half-spin blade grip. Barbara never liked the sensation of being upside down while spinning on the wheel and as they grew older ended up using the wheel of death less and less. Sylvester used to start his act by first facing the target and throwing two knives. He then faced away from the target and again threw two knives. Barbara would then stand up against the board and Sylvester would build a ladder around her using the knives that would be spaced evenly apart from the bottom to the top on each side.

An ad for the Wizards of the Wild West

Irene and Rolf Stey are members of an old Swiss circus family who did a knife act between 1965 and 1985 and made various television appearances, in addition to a performance at the International Circus Festival of Monte-Carlo. They are one of only two acts other than Elizabeth and Collins to have done the simultaneous combination of throwing from a tightrope and the wheel of death.

FRITZ BRUMBACH

Fritz Brumbach from Germany who was billed as The Brumbachs/Los Alamos - a renowned German family act now in its second generation. They began with Fritz Brumbach as thrower and his wife Helga as target girl. Later, daughter Sylvia joined the act as a second target girl and then son Patrick became a thrower. They have made many television appearances. Fritz appeared on *Circus of the Stars* in 1986 with Britt Ekland as his target girl. Fritz and Helga have since retired but Patrick and Sylvia continue the act. Fritz is a Guinness World Record titleholder for rapid throwing around a live target.

PAUL DES MUKE

Paul "Judge" Desmuke was born in 1876. Desmuke was a sideshow performer, justice of the peace, and occasional actor who was remarkable for the fact that he had no arms. Desmuke gained his nickname, Judge, because he became a justice of the peace in Jourdanton, Texas. He later learned to throw knives and worked with the A. G. Barnes Circus and Sideshow and with Zack Miller's Wild West Show. He worked as a double for Lon Chaney in the 1927 silent film *The Unknown*, in which Chaney played an armless knife thrower. Desmuke married a woman named Mae Dixon in 1926, and she worked with him as his target girl in an impalement act that was featured in the Ripley's Odditorium at the "Century of Progress" International Exposition in Chicago in 1933. He is sometimes credited as Peter Dismuki. Desmuke died in 1949.

Elizabeth and Collins

Hungarian thrower Martin Collins had traveled Europe as a circus performer in the 1930s. He met and married Elizabeth around the time of

Advertisement for Elizabeth and Martin Collins

the outbreak of World War II, after spotting her as a potential perform-ing partner. They spent the war years in neutral Sweden and later settled in Britain. Collins developed a signature trick that involved doing the wheel of death stunt while he balanced on a tightrope. Their act took them to nightclubs and vaudeville theaters around the world and they were one of the first impalement acts to break into television. Elizabeth retired from performing in the early 1960s and was replaced by their daughter who was also named Elizabeth (although additionally known as Agnes). Elizabeth and Collins performed on *The Ed Sullivan Show* three times.

STEVE CLEMENTE

Steve Clemente was a Mexican actor known for playing villains in mov-ies and serials in the 1930s. Clemente developed a passion for knife throwing when he was a child. This skill later helped win him act-ing and stunt work in Hollywood and he was trusted to throw knives around movie stars. He appeared in more than sixty movies and threw knives in about ten of them, including *The Sideshow* (1928), *The Mask of Fu Manchu* (1932), *The Gallant Fool* (1933), *Fighting Through* (1934), *Under Two Flags* (1936), *Mad Youth* (1940), *Sing Your Worries Away* (1942), and *Perils of Nyoka* (1942)

We would also like to acknowledge the following knife throwers who have contributed to preserving the history of the art and sport of knife throwing.

Bobby Fairchild; Lew Brotherton; Jay Evans Dan Dennehy, along with his son, John Dennehy; Ben Pitti; Adolfo Rossi; Paul Des Muke; Jack Cavanaugh; Joe Gibson; Augie Gomez; Al Cody; The Shooting Mansfields; Stan Brion; Ivan Thurlow; R. M. Fearnley; Joe Eddy; Bob Fairchild; Jay Evans; Stewart Lipke; John Lepiarz; Arnold R Sandubrase; and Rod Reddwing

Contemporary Professional Knife Throwers

Harry K. McEvoy

Harry McEvoy, considered to be the father of modern day knife throwing was a long time resident of Grand Rapids, Michigan.

He founded Tru-Balance Knife Company in 1949 and was one of the primary suppliers of quality throwing knives to professional and sportsman throwers alike.

He had coached and demonstrated knife and tomahawk throwing for more than forty years and was the founder of the American Knife Throwers Alliance, which is still overseen by knife thrower and knife maker Bobby Branton of Awendaw, South Carolina.

Harry McEvoy was the author of many books on the subject of knife throwing and a few other topics.

He authored such books as *Archery Today, Crusader in the Wilderness, Knife Throwing: A Practical Guide, Knife & Tomahawk Throwing:*

Harry K. McEnvoy, the father of modern day knife throwing

The Art of the Experts, and *For Knife Lovers Only,* and coauthored *Knife Throwing as a Modern Sport,* with Charles Gruzanski.

McEvoy also authored numerous articles in magazines such as *Knife World, Blade, Muzzleloading, Fighting Knives,* and many more too numerous to name.

LARRY CISEWSKI

Larry Cisewski has been billed as the world's greatest knife thrower since 1976, out-performing many professionals on stage and television. He's thought to be one of the most televised knife throwers to date. He has done numerous television spots and talk shows as well as film. He has taught several major actors including Robert DeNiro and Keanu Reeves for films like *The Fan* and *The Matrix.*

Larry Cisewski and his lovely assistant

Che Che White Cloud was born Kenneth Lawrence Pierce, after his father, Lawrence Pierce. He spent his childhood in Shongo, New York, on the Seneca Indian Reservation located near present day Salamanca, New York. He is a mix of Seneca and Onondaga blood of the Hodenosaunee of the Six Nations of the Iroquois Confederacy.

The Pierces aren't an ordinary family, nor do they operate an ordinary business. They are instead a family rich in heritage and tradition with a bloodline that can be traced back at least ten generations of Native Americans. Where the few remaining knife throwers must hold other jobs to pay the bills, Che Che has carried on the family business

Kenneth Pierce or Che Che White Cloud with assistant

Lawrence Pierce or Chief White Cloud practicing some throws.

of throwing battle axes. Also known as Chief White Cloud, Lawrence Pierce had to masquerade as a non-Native American early in his career to get work throwing knives. He often worked with his wife Lillian at a Coney Island Wild West Show around 1915. Here they would throw knives, tomahawks, spears, and boomerangs, as well as performing feats of fast shooting, rope spinning, and trick riding that were started by his great-grandfather, Willet Pierce, three generations ago.

Al Lamarre

Al Lamarre was a friend of mine who used the stage name Chief Golden Eagle and achieved considerable fame as an aerialist with his exceptional balancing skills, as well as his skills with both guns and knife throwing. Lamarre would throw knives at his target while balancing on a rola-bola board. He would often use knives I made for him until his untimely death in the late nineties.

CHIEF GOLDEN EAGLE

KNIVES AND
TOMAHAWK THROWING

Al Lamarre or Chief Golden Eagle hard at work

THE GREAT THROWDINI

The Great Throwdini (a.k.a. Reverend Doctor David Adamovich) started throwing at the age of fifty, following multiple careers that included a professor of exercise physiology, pool hall owner, and ordained minister. He is noted for fast throwing and for reviving the impalement arts amid the magic, modern burlesque, and cabaret scene in New York. He holds thirty-eight world records, mostly for the speed, accuracy, and distance throwing, one of them designated as "one of the Top 100 Guinness World Records of all time." Throwdini has traveled the world bringing his unique interactive style of the impalement arts to huge venues and live television audiences of nearly 100 million people. Of particular note is his return to veiled throwing, having revived the veiled wheel of death in 2010, nearly thirty-five years since it was last performed. To up the ante, he has taken the stunt beyond anyone's imagining. He is the first and only performer to do the Double-Veiled

The Great Throwdini

The Great Throwdini and his assistant at work

Wheel of Death (where two girls are hidden behind a paper veil and spun). His signature closing piece is to stab a signed playing card, previously selected by an audience member. He is a coauthor of one of the few books on the subject of the impalement arts, *A Day on Broadway*, describing, by both himself and his assistant, what it was like to perform the wheel of death for the first time on a Broadway stage.

DICK HAINES

Dick Haines

Dick Haines began to have an interest in knives after he saw a knife-throwing act at his country fair as a boy. Haines eventually went on to start his own show called the Haines Family Circus. The show included the Sky Merchants High Wire with Haines's magic act, fire eating, whips, and of course knife throwing. Having studied and practiced many different professional throwing styles, Haines went on to tutor others in the arts of impalement. At one time he was sending throwing students to the late, great Harry McEvoy for throwing knives and lessons. Haines would tutor over 130 students a year.

His notable tricks include the wheel of death, throws from a rola-bola, and throws through his own lariat loop—sometimes all three at a time! Haines was also the knife thrower for the Great Throwdini's world record blade catch, a whopping twenty-five in one minute.

John Bailey is an ordained, independent, fundamental Baptist Evangelist. He and his wife Monika, go by the stage name of "Lash and Steel Ministries" in their national and international knife throwing and bull-whip performances. He is also a Guinness World Record titleholder.

During his performances he utilizes fifty knives and twelve toma-hawks, and throws them around an assistant from a variety of distances. Twelve items are cut from the assistant's hands in his bullwhip routines. Bailey is also a primary knife-throwing designer for Boker, Germany. He designs are called the TanKri, Starlight, Mini BoKri, Beil-Ax, and the Zeil throwing knife.

John and Monika Bailey

PAUL LaCROSS

LaCross was billed as the world's fastest and fanciest gunslinger and knife and tomahawk thrower. He was also a superb instinct archer and sharpshooter. However, with a full tour of knife-throw-ing events booked in 1990, LaCross had to hang up his knife- and tomahawk-throwing act due to health reasons at the ripe old age of seventy-six. It marked the end of a career that saw him perform

PAUL LA CROSS "WORLD'S FOREMOST KNIFE, TOMAHAWK AND AXE THROWER"

Paul LaCross and his assistant

**An old advertisement showing some
of Paul LaCross's stunts**

all over the world, from the former Soviet Union to New Zealand, and before national television audiences. Almost from the outset, LaCross seemed destined for knife-throwing greatness. Born in St. Albans, Vermont, he learned to throw knives in the Boy Scouts. He said that on long hikes the scouts would throw knives and hatchets at trees to pass the time. He said that even then he must have had the knack because in no time he was landing the knife just where he wanted it. When Paul was eighteen, he saw a sports show featuring a knife-throwing and shooting act performed by a Native American. He knew that he could do the same thing and began working up his own routine. When he realized he could make money at it, he turned it into a career.

LaCross has performed his act at state fairs, rodeos, nightclubs, circuses, shopping plazas, and sport shows. He toured what was then the Soviet Union on an American cultural exchange, Japan for the Expo '70, New Zealand, Canada, Hawaii, and even performed in Carnegie Hall. His television appearances include *The Tonight Show*, the *Merv Griffin* and *Mike Douglas* talk shows, *Thrill Seekers* hosted by Chuck Connors, the *What's My Line?* and *To Tell The Truth* game shows, and hundreds of local television shows. In 1983 he appeared on the *Circus of the Stars*, where he threw knives to outline the body of actress Linda Blair.

He has thrown at just about every female member of his family: his wife Bea; daughters Paula and Betty; granddaughters Bonnie, Tammy and Kim, and even his son Bob. LaCross said that he has had a few accidents while throwing, but nothing serious. One of the worst involved Bea. One of their routines called for her to rap with her hand on the target board where Paul was to throw the knife. Blindfolded, LaCross would zero in on the sound. He heard her knock, but for some reason she thought the knock wasn't loud enough and started to knock again. At that moment Paul threw the knife and the blade went through the board and her arm. She had to go backstage and have the knife pulled out. Luckily, there was a doctor in the audience and Bea wound up with only a few stitches.

Paul's performing days are over now but the thrills and chills he's given scores of knife-throwing fans live on in their memories. The late Harry McEvoy may have said it best of LaCross when he wrote: "Special mention should be made of Paul LaCross. He has performed amazing feats with revolvers, rifles, lumberman longhandled axes, bows and arrows, and best of all, with his sixteen throwing knives and small hatchets. His left-handed style of throwing is unique." He died in August 1993 at the age of seventy-eight.

MIKE & ROSA GROSS

Mike and Rosa Gross perform as "One Sharp Marriage" knife throwers

Mike and Rosa Gross - *One Sharp Marriage* Knife Throwers

Rosa was born in Postellesio, Italy, and moved to America when she was a young girl. Mike grew up in Brooklyn, New York, and moved to Massachusetts as a young boy. They have been married twenty-five years, have raised three children, now grown, and have nine granchildren!

The grandkids are always encouraged to throw knives and tomahawks, and do! Mike and Rosa live in Windsor, Massachusetts, and with their knife-throwing act try to promote trust, love, and forgiveness as being the key to a successful relationship.

Mike and Rosa have been entertaining audiences of all ages since 2001 with knife throwing, crossbow shooting, bullwhip cracking, and the blowgun, performing as "One Sharp Marriage." In 2008, Mike and Rosa were inducted into the International Knife Throwers Hall of Fame located in Austin Texas. They were also named "Outstanding New Performers of the Year" by the IKTHOF that same year. In 2010 and again in 2011 they were named "Knife Throwing Ambassadors of the Year" by the IKTHOF. In 2011, Rosa was named "Target Girl of the Year" and "Female Performer of the Year." Mike was inducted into the Hall of Fame in November of 2012 and named IKTHOF "World Champion Impalement Artist of the Year."

They perform throughout the year at fairs, parties, corporate events, and church functions. They also compete in knife, tomahawk, Mountain Man, bullwhip, atlatl, and blowgun competitions throughout the year. In addition, Mike and Rosa are in high demand as instructors for seminars and demonstrations.

Rose is a crossbow expert. Mike is a certified "Expert" knife thrower by the IKTHOF, a Certified Master Thrown Weapons instructor, and Pro Tour competitor. Mike is world ranked by the IKTHOF in the expert division. A two-time National Knife Throwing Champion, Mike won the IKTHOF/NEUSKTC National Championship in 2009 and was the NE-AKTA National Grand Champion in Knife and Tomahawk for 2011 (his knife and overall score is still the highest recorded scores to date at the NE-AKTA event). Mike is also a two-time National Champion Tomahawk Thrower, winning the 2009 IKTHOF/NEUSKTC National Tomahawk Throwing Championship, and in 2010 won the NE-AKTA National Tomahawk Throwing Championship. In 2009 Mike accomplished a rare feat, winning the "Triple Crown"—finishing first overall in knife, tomahawk, and Mountain Man throws at the IKTHOF National Championship in New Jersey in 2009.

Mike and Rosa have performed three stunts that have never been done before: the inverted wheel of death, the tomahawk catch, and the inverted crossbow shot around a human target. Mike and Rosa's unusual flair for performing death-defying stunts are what sets them apart.

Currently Mike and Rosa are preparing their Wild West Show to include mounted knife and tomahawk throwing as well as mounted shooting on their horse, Trip.

JACK DAGGER

Jack Dagger

Jack Dagger: The King of Fling is a world-renowned knife-throwing comedian (having performed in over 2000 shows). He has been inducted as a Living Legend into the International Knife Throwers Hall of Fame, won three world championships, and has invented the first new knife-throwing stunt in almost a hundred years: The Jack Knife - Cucumber Slice (as seen on the *Tonight Show* with Conan O'Brien).

The King of Fling was recognized by *People* magazine in 2008 as one of the Sexiest Men Alive (in Sexiest A-Z, as "K for Knife Thrower"). He's worked with Nicole Kidman for *Paddington Bear*, with Tim Allen on *Last Man Standing*, on *You Don't Mess with the Zohan* with Adam Sandler, *Monk* with Tony

Shaloub, and *Bones* with David Boreanaz and Emily Deschanel. He was featured on History Channel's *More Extreme Marksmen* as the world's most accurate marksman and an expert in the field of knife throwing, *Top Shot* seasons one through five (and *Top Guns* season one) teaching the competitors how to handle the primitive weapons and providing color commentary, and *Stan Lee's Superhumans* performing seemingly impossible feats of accuracy, garnering him the scientifically measured and confirmed title of Superhuman. Discovery Channel UK also featured Jack in their "Superhuman lab"—measuring his ability to focus with Olympic athlete-level accuracy.

Jack has also appeared in *Vogue Italia* with supermodel Karen Elson on the *MTV Movie Awards*, in the Britney Spears "Circus" music video, on *Good Day LA*, The Learning Channel, and has been featured on both Japanese and Greek television.

In a recent interview, Michael J. Bainton (the executive director of the International Knife Throwers Hall of Fame) said, "I am continuously amazed by his precision marksmanship and his ability to entertain an audience. He is the most accurate knife thrower in the world at this time and constantly raises the standards by which other knife throwers are measured in the entertainment field.

"Although Jack Dagger has retired from competition, he continues to support the expansion of knife throwing as a fun, safe, confidence-building exercise for the general public. He continues to join me and my students at the Alamo to help raise funds for its preservation. Throughout the day he keeps the crowds in stitches with his quick wit and attention to detail. We could use more people like Jack Dagger."

Jack continues to perform in television and film, corporate and trade show environments, renaissance fairs, street festivals (Busker), and fringe festivals all around the world. Jack Dagger is the first professional knife thrower in the world NOT to have a Guinness World Record. This, in and of itself, will eventually be recognized by Guinness.

Originally from Louisiana, Jack now lives in Los Angeles with his beautiful wife Amy and their son Jack Arthur.

Knife History

The knife is man's oldest tool and weapon. No other instrument of civilization has had more historic praise or has undergone so much change over the centuries and is an essential part of our lives even today. In the world that I grew up in, a knife was first and foremost a tool to handle even the most mundane task of the day. The housewife needs a knife to prepare food and to do her daily chores in preparing the family meals. The butcher in the grocery store is useless without his knives. We use small pocket knives or fixed blades to open our mail, open packages, and to cut loose that hanging string on our clothes. Where would our soldiers that we send off to battle in foreign lands be without man's oldest tool? Most were issued knives and bayonets. The knives today are a far cry from the first knives of the caveman.

The first knives were nothing more than pieces of stone with a natural edge. As time went by, an edge was chipped by a stone until it felt good in the hand. Later, an edge was ground on by rubbing the stone against another stone. Little by little, as man evolved, so did the knife. Our predecessors shaped the knife longer and fastened longer handles for more reach and leverage, and then attached even longer handles until they had a spear.

However, man always had that shorter instrument that was soon to become the forerunner of our modern knife. He then felt the need to for an instrument to hold with both hands that he could swing with brute force to finish off crippled game.

The club and stone club were ancestors to the battle axe and the tomahawk. Mankind has evolved to a point that our early ancestors never could have dreamed of—they never would have imagined seeing an electric carving knife or a double bit axe. Down through the ages, cutlery changed from the crude hand hatchet and the flint knife, then the dagger, sword, the meat cleaver, the battle axe, the lance, spear, arrow, and the switchblade. The variety of cutlery at our disposal today is endless. From the Neanderthal man, on through the dark ages, edged weapons played a distinctive part of mankind's evolution.

The daggers that plunged into Julius Caesar or the silent blades that drove the French out of Sicily in 1282 are all part of history.

Weapons and tools have all been known by many names regardless of size, shape, or form. They all have, and do, serve a part of our lives—past, present, and future. Perhaps it is an inherited urge to throw such instruments. It is true that almost all males have that urge. Our lives, our food, the welfare of our family may not depend on the ability to be proficient with a pointed or edged instrument. It is a skilled sport; it is good exercise and it is a lot of fun.

TOMAHAWK HISTORY

There's nothing that stirs the imagination of men and boys like a Kentucky long rifle, a Colt Peacemaker, or perhaps the most recognizable knife of all, the Bowie knife, along with its companion the Tomahawk. We grew up on movies where frontiersmen used these tools in their daily life to perform such tasks as chopping down small trees, defending their family, or hunting small game. It's these films that have helped keep these romantic images fresh in our minds from childhood into adult life.

Tomahawks have been a part of our heritage for over 300 years. They are a type of axe from North America that traditionally resembles a hatchet with a straight shaft made from hickory wood. The name came into the English language in the 17th century as an adaptation of the Powhatan (Virginian Algonquian) word. After man fashioned his first knife from flint, obsidian or stone, he soon felt the need to for an instrument to hold with both hands that he could swing with brute force to finish off crippled game. The club and stone club were ancestors to the battle axe and the tomahawk. The early stone war clubs then evolved to sharpened flat stone war heads, then to chipped flint war heads, and finally to forged steel tomahawks much as we know them today. The early 17th and 18th century English and French traders produced forged steel tomahawks which were used as trade goods for Native Americans. These were readily adopted by the native tribes as utility tools and weapons. Used by Native Americans and European Colonials alike, they were often employed as a hand-to-hand or a thrown weapon.

The tomahawk design was changed quite a bit over time by the Europeans and Americans. Engraved heads were quite common, as were inlays of brass, pewter, and silver. Some tomahawk handles were adorned with beads and horse hair, brass tacks or steel studs. One of the most unique features to appear were the pipe tomahawks that had a bowl at the poll of the tomahawk. These bowls, as well as the handles, were drilled so that one could add tobacco. The pipe tomahawk best symbolizes the tomahawks of that period. Smoking tobacco with another during certain rituals was considered an honor in some tribes. This is what made the tomahawk a fitting symbol for a warrior and someone who always lived as one with their environment.

Other styles of tomahawks include the hammer poll and the spike tomahawk. The hammer poll was just that, a hardened piece of steel that was forged into the design on the back of the poll. It was used for striking and hammering as you would use a hammer today. The spike tomahawk had a sharpened spike forged into the rear of the poll to be used for anything from splitting wood to fighting off wild animals or an aggressor.

It's thought that knife or tomahawk throwing as a pastime started as far back as the Civil War, when soldiers would throw to pass the time around camp. While cleaning and preparing their weapons for battle, they would often partake in a little friendly competition.

It's suspected that the last time the traditional tomahawk was used in combat in the United States was at the battle of Little Bighorn between the Sioux and the 7th Calvary, on June 25, 1876. A more modern version of the weapon would again prove itself in battle more than a hundred years later during the Vietnam War. During this period in our history soldiers used a shorter version of the tomahawk called a LaGana Hawk.

The tomahawk may have been retired from battle, but it lived on through the sixties and early seventies as enthusiasts gathered for "mountain men" themed rendezvous. Today tomahawk throwing is still a popular sport among American historical reenactment groups. There are now hundreds of meet-ups and events that host tomahawk throwing competitions.

CHAPTER 2

SAFETY DISCLAIMER

Knife and tomahawk throwing is a potentially dangerous activity. The individuals associated with this publication cannot and do not have control or responsibility over the actions of the reader. *This information is presented for reference use only.* By reading this publication, the reader agrees to not hold any parties associated with this manual liable for any results or actions directly or indirectly associated with the materials contained within this manual.

Safety first - Stop and think

Observe The Law

Knives, tomahawks, and other edged tools may be regulated by various local law jurisdictions, particularly when viewed as other than sporting or utility equipment. Be advised to research all federal, state, and local restrictions regarding these tools.

Getting Started

Knife Throwing as a hobby

I often have people who will stop and ask me what they should look for when thinking about purchasing a throwing knife. The opinions that I will be offering are mine alone and come from forty-five years as a knife thrower and over twenty-nine years as a custom knife maker.

This is a story that I like to share during my seminars and exhibitions that I attend around the country.

Most guys who are interested in sports or are avid hunters and out-doorsmen have at one time or another either wanted to throw a knife or have wanted to learn how to throw a knife. This is a scenario that I have heard repeated many times throughout my career as a knife maker and knife thrower from guys who seek me out to purchase a quality throw-ing knife or to get some tips on knife throwing.

A father and his son get up early on a Saturday morning and head down to the local gun and knife show. The father and son spend half of the day looking at guns and knives with the son mostly looking over all of the shiny knives offered by the different vendors.

The father, after walking around all morning finally finds a gun that he would like to own and as they begin to leave, he looks around an sees his son still looking at the shiny knives who asks if he can buy a couple of the small throwing knives. The father, feeling a little guilty about buying the gun, eventually buys his son a set of "el cheapo" throwing knives and walks out the door.

Once the father and son get home, the father hides the gun that he just purchased from his wife. His son, who is ready to start throwing knives, is looking for a little guidance from his father.

His father looks around and sees a 4 ft x 8 ft piece of plywood laying by the storage shed and then leans the plywood up against the shed and begins to give his son tips on throwing knives that he had heard from one of his buddies.

After a number of failed attempts and a few bounces that almost got him in the foot, the father takes the knife away from his son and begins to throw the knives himself using the same tips that he had just given his son.

After many attempts to throw the small "el cheapo" knives into the plywood target, he gathers up the knives and tells his son that they aren't good at throwing knives and puts the knives away into the storage drawer never to be seen again.

A few years later, the father and son visit a major knife show where they attend one of my knife-throwing seminars. They watch closely how I am sticking the knives into the target one after another.

After the seminar is over, they come up to say hello and to ask a few questions. They relate a similar story about how they have tried to throw knives, but were no good at it. I usually will invite them up to the throwing line and one-by-one, I get them sticking knives—one-by-one. Now they are armed with the correct information that they need to be successful at knife throwing.

First of all, I like to tell beginners that you need three things in a quality throwing knife.

You need length for control; it will help if it is center-balanced, and it needs weight for penetration. A good rule of thumb is to use the formula created by knife-throwing legend, Harry K. McEvoy.

Harry felt that a knife should weigh approximately 1–1 ¼ ounces for every inch in length. A knife that is at least 12 inches in length will be easier to control because the length with make it turn over a little slower and the length will aid you in achieving a better grip.

A center-balanced knife will be more stable in flight and will allow you to throw the knife by either the handle or blade. A knife made with the above McEvoy formula will have sufficient weight for penetration which is crucial to being able to penetrate a target.

Most good throwing knives should be somewhat pointy and do not need to be extremely sharp. Even bowie knives do not need to be sharp; they only need to have a pointed tip.

I am somewhat biased towards custom throwers because I make custom throwing knives and I've owned hundreds of throwing knives. I can honestly say that I've thrown some of the best, and I've thrown a lot of bad ones too.

I know everything comes down to price. My philosophy is to buy the best set of throwing knives that you can afford. For the price that some people will pay for a good pair of sneakers, you can buy a couple of custom throwing knives. Good custom throwing knives will last a lifetime if you take reasonable care of them and you don't lose them in the weeds.

I guarantee all of my knives for life as long as they were not obviously abused or up to the point where I am no longer able to make them. I have people who have been using my knives for over twenty years and I have seen guys throw older Tru-Balance knives that are forty to fifty years old.

Consider this excellent quote from John Ruskin:

"It's unwise to pay too much but it's unwise to pay too little. When you pay too much you lose a little money that is all. When you pay too little, you sometimes lose everything, because the thing you bought was incapable of doing the thing you bought it to do."

Even though the factories have come a long way in making quality throwers, there are quite a few out there that will work fine for a beginner. When you begin going to knife-throwing tournaments or hanging around with other knife throwers, I believe you will see most of the serious knife throwers using custom throwing knives.

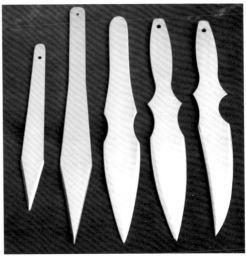

Quality throwing knives made by Bobby Branton

Before you begin

Please take a few minutes to read this article by my friend Dr. Michael J. Bainton

Before starting any exercise program, anaerobic or aerobic, you should consult your health care professional and discuss your exercise program before starting.

Eccentric isotonic exercise, such as what knife throwing entails, is also called "active range of motion exercise." The muscle shortens during isotonic exercise and muscle contraction causes a rise in the heart rate and a marked increase in stroke volume that results in an increase in cardiac output and a net decrease in peripheral resistance (due to vasodilatation of contracted muscles). Isotonic exercise, such as knife throwing, will produce a moderate rise in systolic blood pressure, but the diastolic pressure usually remains unchanged.

Anaerobic exercise is typically used by athletes in non-endurance sports to build power. Muscles that are trained under anaerobic conditions develop biologically differently, giving them greater performance in short duration activities. The contraction and release of muscles from start to finish of a single knife throw is a good example of this. The act of throwing a knife utilizes the entire muscular structure.

Swimming is a very similar exercise in that it utilizes all the muscles of the body. The successful knife thrower develops muscle memory in the consistency of the contraction and release of muscles used in the delivery of the knife.

The anaerobic threshold is the exercise intensity at which lactate starts to accumulate in the bloodstream. This happens when it is produced faster than it can be removed (metabolized). This point is sometimes referred to as the lactate threshold or the onset of blood lactate accumulation.

Knife throwing, unless done in excess of a thrower's fitness level, is an exercise that is normally below the anaerobic threshold, and any lactate produced by the muscles is removed by the body without it building up. It is advisable to include an aerobic regime with your daily knife-throwing activities such as walking, cycling, or swimming to increase proper breathing techniques and for a general increase in general fitness.

The anaerobic threshold is a useful measure for deciding exercise intensity. Not overdoing either the anaerobic value of knife throwing or the aerobic value of walking, swimming, or other activities that will use a large amount of oxygen and gross muscle movement, is important. Soreness or blood lactate accumulation will soon disappear with a consistently increasing workout regimen.

In other words, start out slow and increase your throwing and your choice of aerobic exercise in a systematic manner. Throwing one hundred knives from half or one spin and walking a half a mile for a few days is recommended to get you started to stay below your lactate threshold.

If you have had a sedentary lifestyle, an increase every three to four days in both the anaerobic and aerobic exercises should suffice to build your endurance to the desired level when starting knife throwing.

A great backyard target setup shown
by my friend, Bill Cantey

A four-inch-thick cross section of a pine tree
works great as a practice target.

A professional target board for performances.

AKTA-style competition range

Brenda Branton throwing tomahawks on a AKTA regulation target range

Typical setup for competition in a room to help minimize damage to the event venue

Mountain Man style target that can be easily built for the backyard

Targets and Construction

Having a good target can make a big difference in whether or not you have a good experience throwing knives or a bad one. Most beginners will try to find the easiest type of target to set up quickly so that they can begin throwing immediately. A good target needs to be sturdy to withstand the rigors of throwing knives and tomahawks that can weight a little over one pound each. A flimsy target can work to your disadvantage by not letting you get a good solid stick like you would normally get in a more rigid target.

The best types of woods to use to build a quality target are pine, cottonwood, redwood, or any of the softer woods. Just try to steer clear of woods that are either too soft or too hard. You will have to learn what type of trees are indigenous to your area and seek them out. The easiest way to get log rounds suitable for throwing knives and tomahawks is to search for tree-clearing services in your phone book, or pay attention to tree crews that are taking down trees after a storm or clearing trees for a new subdivision. You can usually pay them a few dollars for the trees and they will cut them to size for you. I generally like to get my log rounds cut to about a minimum of 20 inches in diameter measuring across the face of the log and somewhere around four to six inches thick. Four inches is great for knives, but six inches works great for tomahawks and axes.

Once you find a source and have the targets in hand, there are a lot of ways that you can build a sturdy target. I have tried many ways and have come up with one design that is not expensive to build and will last many years with very little maintenance.

The design that I have on my knife- and tomahawk-throwing range is made for 4" x 6" x 8' treated lumber and a section of 2" x 6" wide piece of lumber.

I like to take the two 8-foot-long pieces of 4" x 6" treated lumber and bury them into the ground and pour a bag of concrete around them to make them good and sturdy. Make sure that you level them and space them around three to four feet apart. You will then take your 2" x 6" piece of lumber and mark off approximately 48 inches from the ground and center the board on your mark and nail it to the two 4" x 6" upright pieces that are secured into the ground. You should now have a structure resembling an "H" shape.

After everything is secured properly and you have a nice rigid setup, I like to drill two 3/8-inch holes in the middle of the 2" x 6" piece so that you can lag bolt your log round to the 2" x 6" cross piece from the rear. After you drill your holes in the cross piece, have someone lift the target around and center it in the cross piece and take two 3/8" x 2"-long lag screws with a washer and screw them into the rear of the target using a ratchet and socket.

HOW TO THROW A KNIFE

I think almost every man has had the dream where he could pick up any knife and hurl it into the target. We all seem to get dazzled by the cool blockbuster films in Hollywood or the old spaghetti westerns where the bad guy would rob a bank and jump on his horse while trying to escape. While the bad guy is moving away from the cowboy in the street, the cowboy draws his bowie knife from its scabbard and hurls it towards the bad guy moving away from him on the horse and sticks the knife square in the back—and he falls dead off the horse. He may have gotten a lucky shot from 10 feet away, but when the horse is traveling further and further away, the odds of him even getting close are pretty slim. With a little training and guidance by a competent knife thrower, it is really not that hard to stick a knife into the target. The method that I am going to show is MY way of throwing and teaching. This is not rocket science and some people like to make it look harder than it is. I have trained and showed thousands of people of all ages and from all walks of life how to throw knives and tomahawks. My goal when I teach is to give you instant gratification. I want you to be able to stick the knife into the target as soon as possible. When you get that first good stick, it gives you a good boost of confidence and it gives me a good idea of how far you need to be from the target for a person of your size and athletic ability.

I like to try to keep things simple. There is no need to make this any harder than it needs to be, so I'll try to break this down so that we can have you sticking knives as quickly and as safely as possible. If you can throw a baseball or cast a fishing rod, you should be able to throw a knife. You will be using the same motion and body mechanics in knife and tomahawk throwing. Once you make a few sticks into the target and feel comfortable with your throw, you can play around with your grip so that it is even more comfortable to you. There is nothing more satisfying to hear the "thunk" as you stick your first knife into the target.

As a rule of thumb, for an average person you will need to mark a spot anywhere from 10 to 12 feet away from the target and that will be where you make your first attempt at throwing a knife.

Once you get a nice quality throwing knife like I mentioned earlier, you want to hold it in your hand by the handle with the tip of the blade pointing forward. I want you to hold the knife in your hand with only about a half inch of the handle sticking out the rear. I want you to grip the knife like you are going to hammer a nail or chop wood with the knife. As you are standing there preparing for your first throw (assuming that you are right handed), I want you to stand on the line with your left foot placed right behind the mark that you have made on the ground. You should be very relaxed with your right foot slightly back, and you should be balanced so that you do not fall. As you begin to wind up for the throw, you should bend your knee slightly and rock back and forth ever so slightly. Carefully raise the knife to the rear just behind your head on your right side, and as you begin to bring your right hand forward, slowly bend the left knee as I mentioned earlier. Just before your right arm extends fully, gently let the knife slide out of your right hand and gently open your hand as the knife is released. The knife should spin one complete revolution and stick into the target.

Just like swinging a baseball bat or swinging a golf club, you want to let your arm follow through as the knife leaves your hand.

Finally, practice, practice, practice!!!!

MECHANICS OF THE THROW

THE GRIP

The grip on the knife or tomahawk can be either the hammer grip or the modified hammer grip as illustrated in the following figures. The hammer grip is the same grip used when grasping the handle of a hammer or similar tool. With this grip, the thumb wraps around and lies on the side of the handle.

The blade grip is used to throw distances that involve half-turns. The grip is essentially the same for a handle grip with the exception of grasping the blade end of the knife. This may seem awkward at first but is easily overcome with practice. *Do not use sharpened knifes with this grip.*

Hammer Grip
FIGURE 2A

Blade Hammer Grip
FIGURE 2B

Normally, all the fingers contact and wrap around the handle as well. The modified hammer grip is the same with the exception of the thumb being placed on the near edge, spine, or back of the knife blade or tomahawk handle. The grip is firm but not tight, allowing the knife or tomahawk and hand to part smoothly when released.

Modified Hammer Grip

FIGURE 2C

THE STANCE

FIGURE 2D

NOTE: This discussion is for right-handed throwers. Left-handed throwers should substitute "left for right" and "right for left" in the text to convert the instruction for left-handed throwing.

The *Professional Style* of throwing is done without a step into the throw. The throw is executed from a modified standing position (Fig. 2D). The rear foot may move forward to the position of the forward foot as the follow-through of the throw is completed.

1. **Foot placement** - The left foot toe is placed on the distance mark. The throwing side right foot is a comfortable distance behind the left foot (about two feet), and nearly in line with the forward foot and target, but slightly to the right of the left foot.
2. **The knees** should be flexed somewhat to provide ease of shifting the body weight forward during the throw.
3. **The knife or tomahawk** is held in the right hand in front of the thrower at about chest level. The left hand may steady the throwing hand. The elbows should not be resting on the stomach or sides, but out in front of the thrower's body and spaced somewhat less than shoulders' width apart.
4. **The aim** is most generally that of picking a spot on the target and bringing the hands and knife or tomahawk to the position where your eye(s), the knife or tomahawk, and the target spot are all in line. This is the position the thrower assumes for concentration, consistent repetition, and familiarization in execution of the throw.

THE WINDUP

FIGURE 2E

5. **The windup** starts by bringing the throwing hand back alongside the head. The throwing hand should be directly over the right shoulder (Fig. 2E).

6. **The body** rocks back slightly while the left arm is extended towards the target aiming point. The throwing arm continues a backward motion to the "*cocked*" position (Fig. 2F).

THE THROW

FIGURE 2G

The throw requires two movements involving accelerating and delivering the knife or tomahawk.

7. **The lunge** starts by a forward motion of the right throwing arm. At the same time, the left arm begins to swing down and rearwards, and the body shifts forward (Fig. 2G).
8. **The release** is performed as the right throwing arm is in full forward motion and at the apex of the right arm's movement relative to the ground. At this time the body weight has shifted more to the left foot; the right foot may leave the ground slightly, and the left arm has begun to swing behind the throwers body (Fig. 2H).

THE FOLLOW THROUGH

FIGURE 2I

9. **The follow-through** is completed by the smooth continued movement of the right throwing hand coming to stop as if reaching for the ground (Fig. 2I), the left arm continuing its rearward motion to counterbalance the forward lean (Fig. 2J), and the right foot coming to rest near the left forward foot to regain balance (Fig. 2K).

FIGURE 2J

FIGURE 2K

KNIFE THROWING METHOD VARIATIONS

As mentioned previously, there are many variations to the *Professional Style* of knife throwing. The following descriptions detail the most common of these variations from a right-handed context.

Step from - This is the same motion as the *Professional Style* except the thrower is one step behind his distance mark with the right foot forward in the ready stance. A full step forward is taken with the left foot, which places the left foot on the distance mark and the throw is delivered. This variation allows the thrower to use forward body motion to add to the velocity of the throw, thus producing a greater impact force.

Step into - This is the same motion as the *Professional Style* except the thrower is a short step behind his distance mark with the left foot forward in the ready stance. A short step forward is taken with the left foot, which places the left foot on the distance mark and the throw is delivered. This variation adds little to the throw but may be a more comfortable motion for the thrower.

Feet together - The thrower places both feet on the distance mark at a comfortable distance apart to deliver the throw. This is an awkward variation for most who try this style.

Lift rear foot/strong follow-through - This is the same motion as the *Professional Style* except the thrower extends the follow-through to the point where the entire body weight is shifted to the forward left foot and the rear right foot leaves the ground. The throw is delivered at maximum speed and power. This variation is very much like the windup, stretch, and delivery of the professional baseball pitcher's fastball. It allows the thrower to use maximum forward body motion to add to the velocity of the throw, thus producing a much greater impact force. It is worth mentioning that using greater force and higher velocity throws usually do not produce greater accuracy.

Reversed footing - With this stance the right foot is placed forward on the distance mark with the left foot a comfortable distance behind. This is an awkward and unnatural stance to throw from, but a few individuals have used and won major competitions with this form.

THE BASICS OF THROWING A TOMAHAWK

The feel and flight characteristics of the tomahawk are the most notable and considerable differences from that of the knife. The design of the tomahawk is inherently heavy at the end of the head. This makes for a seemingly awkward feel when throwing as compared to the relatively center-balanced knife. Most throwers rapidly become familiar with this weight and size difference and adjust accordingly.

The weight of the tomahawk is both an advantage and a disadvantage. The disadvantage of the greater weight is that it must be carried if used as a camping tool as well as a thrower. Gratefully, as competitors, we do not carry our implements on our bodies over long distances or periods of time, but instead set them down between rounds of throwing. The advantage of the greater weight is that the tomahawk has greater impact force and therefore does not require a strong throw. The weight of the tomahawk does most of the work for the thrower, leaving only distance and accuracy to be concerned with.

To achieve full-turn throws, the tomahawk's blade edge must be facing forward toward the target. Pace out six normal steps from the target and face it. This should put you at 14 to 16 feet from the target for one turn. Throw the tomahawk using the motions described in the *How to Throw a Knife* section, but use more of a downward chopping motion for the lunge/throw. Observe the position of the handle of the stuck tomahawk. If the handle hits first and the tomahawk bounces off the target, is touching the target, or nearly parallel with the target, step back six inches and try again. If the handle is perpendicular with the target or the tomahawk hits headfirst and bounces off the target, step forward six inches and try again. Continue to adjust the distance until you get a consistent stick with the handle pointing *down* at 45 degrees. This is the optimum stick position.

To achieve half-turn throws, the tomahawk's blade edge must be facing rearward toward your face. Pace out six normal steps from the target, add three more steps for the half-turn, and face the target. This should put you at 18 to 22 feet from the target for a one-and-a-half turn throw. Throw and adjust as described above until you get an optimum stick position with the handle pointing *up* at 45 degrees.

NO-SPIN THROWING

What has increasingly become known as no-spin throwing has been popularized by a friend of mine who uses the pen name, Ralph Thorn. Ralph began by making videos showing his style of throwing from a variety of distances, and not long thereafter, wrote a book on the subject along with a companion DVD. The Thorn style, as it has become known, is pure and simple instinct throwing. Once you catch on, it is a fun style to learn. The hardest part of learning the Thorn style of throwing is trying to unlearn years of conventional spin throwing that has a totally different way of releasing the knife.

An experienced no-spin knife thrower such as Ralph Thorn will be able to pick up any knife and immediately feel the weight and balance of that knife and adjust his throw accordingly. I read his research on finding the optimal balance point for no-spin throwing, and Ralph has developed a formula to assist you in being able to find the balance point on most throwing knives—to no-spin. As a student of Ralph Thorn and his method of no-spin throwing, I will be discussing techniques and give observations based on his teachings.

There are several varieties of the no-spin or "quarter-spin" as some people like to call it. There is a Japanese style, a Russian style, and the American or "Thorn" style, as well as other variations. They have probably existed for a long time but only over the last decade have they become well-known to the public.

Conventional knife throwers always knew about the no-spin underhand throw, in which the knife is gripped as for conventional knife throwing and shot forward underhand using a stiff elbow and wrist and a sudden release action—where the hand is thrown suddenly open. And some people used a "palm" style for close-range no-spin throwing that is a sort of variation on the no-spin underhand—only swinging the arm overhand and chopping downwards, instead of upwards, before releasing. But the new styles are different.

There are some style and grip variations within the modern no-spin style, but one thing the new styles all have in common is a certain grip that is different from the conventional knife-throwing grip. Some people call it the "finger of God" grip, after the painting on the Sistine Chapel that sort of resembles this grip.

In the basic no-spin grip, the knife is held with the plane of the blade vertical, as with the conventional knife-throwing style. But the plane of the wrist is different. In no-spin throwing the wrist is aligned horizontally, parallel to the ground, instead of held more vertically as in conventional knife throwing. In no-spin throwing the index finger is placed on the top edge of the knife, with the thumb on the flat of the handle, and the other three fingers cupped around and under the handle.

As with conventional throwing, you can choke up or down to adjust the location of the balance point, which will change the way the weight of the knife feels in your hand. Thorn says when he throws conventional throwing knives he generally prefers them to have the weight more on the handle side, but no-spin throwers are adaptable and some prefer center-balanced knives.

In terms of arm and body movement, no-spin throwers typically have a throwing style that resembles throwing a baseball or a football a little more than it resembles conventional knife throwing. Some of them even throw sidearm. But they don't release a knife like a ball—they release earlier. The main key to the no-spin throw is to release the knife while the point is still pointing at the sky. If the grip is correct and the release is timed right, the force of gravity will immediately start to pull the point of the knife towards the ground. In other words, the knife begins pointing at twelve o'clock but ends at three o'clock, sticking into the target. That's why some people call it the quarter-spin. But this point drop happens gradually, like an arrow shot at a high angle, losing its force over a long distance and eventually hitting the ground. No one calls an arrow's flight a quarter-spin, so we have always preferred the term "no-spin."

There is a different technique for throwing no-spin from close range and from longer range, say beyond 12 feet or so. From close range the release is later and you can use more wrist action to propel the knife. The use of wrist action is associated especially with the self-defense oriented Thorn style and creates a lot of interesting throwing angles and a lot of power. It also allows you to throw larger weapons, even full size swords. But from further back it doesn't work as well.

From long range or when using very small knives or the other weapons that are used—anything from shuriken spikes to screwdrivers—no-spin throwers tend to use a more "frozen" wrist (though still with the hand cupped more over the top of the knife, instead of to the side of the knife as with conventional throwing) and can also keep the elbow stiff as well. The release action is even earlier as no-spin throwers get further from the target and the release gets more and more like a knuckleball in baseball or a "shot put" action, where the fingers don't stroke the handle a little on release as they would with a fastball or in the close-range no-spin throw.

From a longer range many no-spin throwers generate more power by dipping their front knee and turning their torso quickly on their front hip as they push off the back foot, using the shoulder as a pivot and turning the arm into a sort of whip. If you're having trouble visualizing this, it looks quite a bit like a baseball pitcher's windup and throwing action, though the arm is kept a little stiffer. This makes the release slower but generates velocity, and that helps increase range with the no-spin. The faster a knife moves, the less time it has for the point to drop, extending the no-spin flight pattern over a greater distance.

The no-spin style is more of an instinctive style, based more on a feel for the weight of the knife than a formula. There is also an interesting half-spin variation on the no-spin, which uses the same basic grip and release, except the knife is held by the blade. The idea is to control the rate of spin you put on the knife, making it spin a little faster to stick in a near target and a little slower to hit one further back. This, of course, takes a lot of practice in judging distance and figuring out just how much spin to put on the knife.

No-spin throwing has had an upsurge in popularity over the last few years. It is mostly associated with martial arts and self defense but has a recreational aspect as well. No-spin throwing even pops up sometimes in conventional knife-throwing events, which can be pretty diverse, and some people are looking to establish rules for contests.

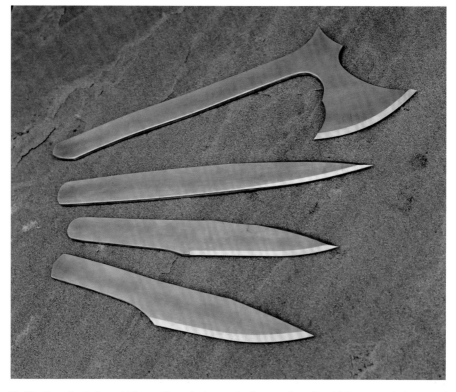

Quality throwing knives widely used by today's no-spin throwers from Patrick Brewster of Flying Steel

CHAPTER 3

COMPETITIVE KNIFE THROWING

COMPETITION KNIFE THROWING HISTORY

In 1964 Chuck Gruzanski enlisted the help of long-time knife maker and knife- thrower Harry K. McEvoy of Grand Rapids, Michigan, to form a new knife-throwing organization, the Tru-Flyte Knife Throwers of America. This was to be the very first national organization founded to promote knife throwing as a modern sport. The board of consultants included Harry K. McEvoy, Robert Abels, William D. Randall Jr., Gary Randall, Robert Lee Wilson, Gil Hibben, Ralph H. Totsch, Paul LaCross, L. Garg, Norman C. Heilman Jr., Jim Ramsey, Kenneth Pierce, and Tumio Mawa. Each one of these men were true pioneers and craftsmen.

Chuck decided to publish a bimonthly publication entitled *The Knife Thrower*. Due to this publication being financed out of his pocket, it would only be published for a total of seven issues. Tru-Flyte Knife Throwers of America seemed to be a little ahead of its time and only lasted for a couple of years.

In 1971 when he felt the time was right again for another new organization, Harry K. McEvoy founded the American Knife Throwers Alliance (AKTA). With the help of Carmen Corrado of the world famous

Corrado Cuterly Store in Chicago, the AKTA grew to have a national membership of more than twelve hundred enthusiastic sportsmen knife throwers. A quarterly newsletter, *The Bullseye Buster*, published twenty-two issues before publication had to be suspended. With very limited help and facilities, it became too large to produce and mail. Among the many things it accomplished, its primary goals were to provide a blueprint for organizing competitions at a local level, to offer guidelines for competition, and to serve as a clearing house for information concerning all aspects of the sport. The AKTA was, and is, dedicated to promoting the art of knife throwing as a sport, recreation, and a hobby.

Bobby Branton has a deep and rich history with Harry K. McEvoy and the Tru-Balance Knife Company. Back when Bobby had begun to make knives, he was searching for information on what made a quality throwing knife. He stumbled upon Harry McEvoy, owner of the Tru-Balance Knife Company of Grand Rapids Michigan. The two became friends and Harry mentored Bobby on his formula for what made a quality throwing knife. After a lot of snail mail correspondence, Bobby decided to make his own line of throwing knives and asked his knife-throwing mentor Harry, if he could pay him to design his first line of throwers. With McEvoy's support and encouragement, Bobby went on to design and add to that line of knives. In the late eighties, McEvoy was looking at serious retirement and had plans to sell his world famous Tru-Balance Knife Company. After a few years, both franchises became defunct and Bobby purchased the assets and rights to one of these companies but went on to develop and market his line of throwers with hopes of one day being able to bring this company back to life.

Shortly after that, McEvoy passed away after a brief illness. When the news reached Bobby, he called to talk with family members whom he had never met and found out that Harry's son, Stephen, had worked very closely with his father over the years. Bobby was told that Stephen would be carrying on the family business of making throwing knives. A friendship quickly developed between Stephen and Bobby who began to correspond frequently and became very close. After being entrenched into the knife-throwing scene and with his desire to preserve and promote knife throwing, Bobby began collecting the older Tru-Balance Knives and had amassed a large collection. One day while talking to Stephen, Bobby received Stephen's blessings to bring back the old knife-throwing organization that his father had founded, known as The American Knife Throwers Alliance.

After consulting with his wife, Brenda, and longtime professional knife-thrower Che Che Whitecloud, and Stephen, Bobby held the first all knife-throwing tournament that had been held in the United States in years. It was a huge success and the AKTA is still going strong with its original mission of promoting and preserving the art of knife throwing and a sport and hobby. They never wanted to be in the business of strictly promoting tournaments.

In 2007 after eleven years of hosting world class knife throwers and tournaments, Bobby decided to suspend all AKTA events due to the time constraints required in running a full-time knife business and trying to keep up with his growing membership. He had come to the conclusion

AKTA style target set up for competition

that they had done their part in becoming the catalyst for new knife-throwing groups and organizations who would carry the torch in promoting knife-throwing tournaments. The AKTA still holds an annual AKTA-style event yearly in Pennsylvania hosted by their tournament director, Joe Darrah, who is a world class knife thrower in his own right.

In 2003, Mike Bainton founded the International Knife Throwers Hall of Fame (IKTHOF) in Austin, Texas, in September 2003. The IKTHOF, of which Bobby is proud to have been inducted as "Knife Thrower of the Year" in 2004, provides a positive influence and professional service to its members. Founder and executive director, Dr. Michael J. Bainton, PhD, has based the IKTHOF headquarters in the central United States in Austin, Texas. The association is dedicated to increasing the communication, education and recognition of all knife throwers. It is designed to service the varied needs and interests of members from all knife-throwing styles.

The very first AKTA competition in 1996

Modern knife- and tomahawk-throwing organizations such as the American Knife Throwers Alliance (AKTA) and the International Knife Throwers Hall of Fame (IKTHOF) use the following rules and guidelines below. These guidelines will be applicable to both knife-throwing and tomahawk-throwing events. I have tried to give you an idea of the different rules used by the different organizations because we all have the same goals but have different ideas on how to get there.

- I like to have at least 25 feet on all sides of the target set up. This will allow for bounces and will give you ample warning should a child or stray pet wander into the area. Once you have more than one person, you can rotate, with each acting as a Range Officer to keep an eye out for anybody entering the range area. Roping off the area with a roll of reflective tape will assist you in making sure everyone knows the boundaries.

**Knife-making and knife-throwing legend Dan Dennehy
taking a break at the 1998 AKTA National Championships**

- Make sure that a first aid kit is readily available in case of an accident.
- Have plenty of water available so that you can stay hydrated during your event.
- Make sure there are restrooms or portable restroom facilities available.
- Do not allow alcoholic beverages on the premises. Throwing knives and alcohol do not mix. Have a separate time set aside after the event for socializing.
- Anyone exhibiting unsportsmanlike conduct will be asked to leave the contest site.
- Practice sessions are not mandatory and may be subject to time constraints. Practice sessions will be held at the discretion of the contest holder.
- Before each competition, have a throwers meeting to go over the rules and to make sure that everyone understands them. Let the knife throwers ask questions regarding the rules so that they are clear. Never change the rules without advanced notice. If something should arise that needs immediate attention, I ALWAYS ask the participants if the change will be OK, and 100 percent of the participants have to be in agreement in order to make the temporary change for that event.
- There will be a Range Officer in charge of the throwing range during all practice sessions and competitions. The Range Officer's main responsibility is to ensure safety during practice sessions and competitions, to score the throwers knives or tomahawks, and to watch for throwers who step over the line which can result in a penalty. Anyone disagreeing with the Range Officer can protest his call to the protest committee. The protest committee will consist of two of the highest ranking members that are present. The third man will break a tie, should that occur.

Scoring

- No contestant will be allowed to interfere with the scorekeeper while the contest is underway.

- All recorder scores will be totaled by the scorekeeper and then immediately retotaled by a club official.

- Each contestant will be required to sign a release of liability to compete.
- The general seating area must be roped off and be at least 25 feet behind the ropes.
- No alcohol or drugs are to be consumed before or during a contest.
- No foul language
- Every contest must have a first aid kit available to the contestants.
- Anyone not complying with the safety rules will be asked to leave the contest site.

KNIFE THROWING COMPETITION RULES

(AKTA STYLE)

- Targets will be 5 points.
- Each target should be a 16-inch diameter log round (or painted boards) with a 4-inch diameter bull's-eye worth 5 points. An 8-inch diameter secondary ring is worth 4 points, and a 16-inch diameter outside ring is worth 3 points.
- Targets may be numbered or lettered to define throwing pattern or a predetermined order may be set up prior to start of throw at host's discretion.
- Knives may be 9 inches in length minimum to a total length of 16 inches maximum. This will give those people with smaller knives that they are comfortable with some leeway along the closer distances.

- The target heights should be about knee height for the bottom rounds and about shoulder height for the top rounds on an average sized man or 24 inches for the bottom and 67 inches for the top.
- As a general rule, this would be the bottom and top of the log rounds respectively.
- There will be four distances that knives will be thrown from; these are *minimum* distances and you may stand anywhere behind these lines for your throw but not in front of these lines.
- Distances are 7 feet, 10 feet, 13 feet, and 16 feet which will be a required half spin, one full spin, one-and-half spins, and two full spins respectively.
- Anyone standing over or stepping over the lines will have that throw count as zero after a suggested two verbal warnings by line judge/scorer.
- All throws must be by the blade or handle as per distance requires.
- There will be a total of sixty knives thrown—five knives from each of the four distances, three times, for a highest possible score of 300 points.
- In case of any disputes or questions, another designated person or thrower will be asked to confirm the scoring.
- The highest point ring cut will scored; knives may not be touched by thrower until they have been scored.
- Any thrower touching the knives before scoring will have that throw count as zero after a suggested two verbal warnings by line judge/scorer.

TOMAHAWK THROWING COMPETITION RULES

(AKTA STYLE)

- These rules apply to American Knife Throwers Alliance (AKTA) competition rules.
- Tomahawks will have a minimum handle length of 12 inches from bottom of handle to top of handle or the part that is in line with the

handle in cases where all metal or plastic/composite handled hawks/axes are used with a maximum cutting edge of no more than four and a half inches along the curve of the blade.

- The AKTA will allow the one-piece, all-metal axes such as the Hibben, Condor, SOG, or similarly constructed one-piece axes as long as they fall within the length and width parameters required.
- There will be four hawks thrown at the outer four targets (leaving the center target unused) at only the 13 foot distance, five times for a total of twenty hawks for a possible total point score of 100 points.
- No thrower may step over the line to throw and the same warning rules are suggested for this event as well.
- The person with the highest accumulated points from both knife and hawk will be considered the overall winner of the throw.
- The newcomer who has the highest combined score for both knives and hawks would be considered the winner of the newcomer event.

The event holder will be responsible for any/all trophies or other categories (i.e., second place, third place or children's categories), but the AKTA will help promote any AKTA-sanctioned throw on their site as well as offer logistical advice and when possible offer stickers, patches, or certificates and possibly an occasional prize knife/knives when available.

Any other event such as Mountain Man games, obstacle course, escape and evasion courses, long distance, woods walk, or any other games or challenges will be totally at the discretion of the event

CHAPTER 4

KNIFE-THROWING GAMES

To give the reader an idea of the different types of additional games that can be included in a knife- and tomahawk-throwing competition, here are a few games that are extra events at IKTHOF-style competitions.

All categories expert, intermediate, and novice throwers will throw three tomahawks at three targets moving back to next distance after each three tomahawks, from five distances for a total of sixty tomahawks. Participants will throw a total of fifteen hawks per session from five distances on four separate ranges. Minimum distances are one full spin—three meters handle down, blade facing forward before throwing; a one-and-a-half rotation spin—four meters handle up, blade facing back before throwing; a double spin—five meters handle down, blade facing forward before throwing; a two-and-a-half rotation spin—seven meters handle up, blade facing backwards before throwing; a triple rotation spin—nine meters handle down, blade facing forward before throwing. Tomahawks must be at least 13 inches in length from the end of the handle to the poll of the hawk.

LONG DISTANCE KNIFE

Throwers will qualify from beyond the 5 meter or 16 ft 5 in line. One stick out of three knives is required to continue. All throwers will have numbers. The lowest qualifying number will throw first and will throw three knives at the target from beyond the highest distance of the longest qualifying throw. One knife of the three is all that is required to set a new distance. The next qualifier will throw beyond that distance until a winner is determined.

LONG DISTANCE TOMAHAWK

Participants will throw from beyond the 7 meter line. One stick out of three hawks is required to continue. All throwers will have numbers. The lowest qualifying number will throw first and will throw three hawks from beyond the highest distance of the longest qualifying throw. One hawk of the three is all that is required to set a new distance. The next qualifier will throw beyond that distance until a winner is determined.

Fast Draw

Two throwers will start and both hands must be held shoulder high in front of each thrower. Upon the command of "Go", each thrower will pull his or her knife from the belt around the thrower's waist and throw at the target in front of them. The first knife to hit the target successfully will win. Throwers will continue to throw until one of the contestants sticks the knife in the target. The loser of the competition between the two contestants is out of the contest. The winner of the two contestants will move to the back of the line of waiting throwers. At no time can any thrower change position in the waiting line after the range master has placed you in line or after you have won a heat. To do so would mean disqualification.

Speed Throw

The thrower will on the command of "Go" throw as many knives into a single target as possible from the half-spin distance in a total of twenty seconds.

Silhouette Throw

The throwers will throw on a flat board around a paper cut-out mannequin. There are fifteen 4-inch bull's-eyes around the mannequin. The thrower must start on the lower left bull's-eye and progress up and hit each consecutive bull's-eye. If a thrower misses a bull's-eye, he must throw at the next bull's-eye. In other words if a thrower is throwing at the number two bull's-eye or the second bull's-eye from the bottom and misses, he must now throw at the next bull's-eye to score. Total amounts of points is 75; there are 5 points for each bull's-eye hit in the proper order.

TEXAS THREE STEP

A bowie knife or period knife with a minimum length of 12 inches will be required for the knife throw. The knife handle must be made of leather, wood, or bone. Each participant will throw at one throwing block with the standard IKTHOF point scoring. The thrower will throw 3 knives from sheath to target from one spin behind the 3 meter mark; each participant will then move to the two spin behind the 5 meter mark and throw three knives sheath to target. Each participant will then move behind the 7-meter mark and throw three knives sheath to target. Any throw offs will be judged from the two spin or beyond the 5-meter mark with a total of three knives. Once the thrower has started his/her throw with his/her hand on the handle, the throw must be a fluent motion, never stopping until the knife has left the thrower's hand. One warning will be given should the knife stop and not be thrown in one continuous motion. Upon being told the second time by the judge, the score will not count if there is any hesitation in the throw. From sheath to target, throwing must be accomplished in one continuous motion. Total amount of points is 45.

TEXAS HURRICANE

Three bowie knives or period knives with a minimum length of 12 inches will be required for the knife throw. The handle or scales of the knife must be made out of leather, wood, or bone. Each participant will throw at three 6-inch bull's-eyes on one target starting on the left hand side. The thrower will start with his hand on the first sheathed knife. Upon the command of "Go" the time will start The thrower will pull his first knife and throw it at the first bull's-eye on the left; immediately following the thrower will then pull the second knife and throw it at the middle bull's-eye. Immediately following, the thrower will pull the third knife from the sheath and throw it at the third bull's-eye. The thrower's time will stop when the third knife hits the target. There are 5 points awarded for each knife in the appropriate bull's-eye. For each missed bull's-eye five seconds will be added on to the time. The winner will be determined by the highest number of points and the shortest time period.

How to Start a Knife- and Tomahawk-Throwing Club

After you have been throwing knives and tomahawks for a while, you will begin to meet new people who also share the same interest as you. It may be your next door neighbor who peeks over the fence while you are throwing a few knives, or it could be the guy at the local gun shop or sporting goods store that you struck up a conversation with while looking around in his knife department.

You can have a fun competition with two people. My wife and I often go outside to throw a little in the afternoon, and after we get warmed up a bit, we break out the clipboard with the score sheets.

With the Internet and social media available to us these days, it is easy to get caught up in the larger contests and to try to get knife and tomahawk throwers to come to visit or join your new club. It just is not possible for a lot of people to travel great distances for a one or two day event.

Once you get more than a couple of throwers in your backyard, depending on your location, you may want to look around for some property that the owner would be willing to let you use in order to accommodate more throwers and to have more room in general.

This is up to each group. You may want to look at purchasing some liability insurance once the club gets to a certain size in order to have the added protection against any unforeseen events.

I always suggest that newcomers who are ready to take the next step towards building a new club do so locally. By locally I mean putting up flyers in the local gun shops, archery shops, and sporting goods stores (ask for permission first). Get the word out by word-of-mouth, and before you know it, you will be adding a new thrower here and there until you have a nice group. By all means utilize social media and a website. Try to focus on your town and the next town over. Then expand to other areas of the state and then maybe the neighboring state. You

Knife- and Tomahawk-throwing expert, Stephen D. McEvoy of Tru-Balance Knife Company

may be surprised at how many people you will draw once you get a few meetings and events under your belt.

Sit down with your fellow throwers and write out a mission statement so that everyone can see what the club is about.

Establish a hierarchy of president, vice president, etc., so that the new throwers can have someone to come to ask questions.

Set goals for the club. One goal to be to have a certain number of members. Another goal can be to have one or more throwers represent the club at a major event.

Make up a membership packet for the new members with a membership card and a set of rules that you will be using at your event. Make sure that any rules that are changed be published as soon as possible before an event to make sure that everyone is aware of the changes. Try not to make changes to the rules at least thirty days prior to an event.

Have someone designated as a secretary in case you decide to ask for the throwers to pay dues to belong to the club. The secretary can take notes of your meetings and remind club members of important items and can serve as club photographer to document your club's progress and growth.

Have a few minutes for a show-and-tell so that each member (especially the new ones) can see what style or brand of knife and tomahawk the seasoned veteran throwers are using.

Set aside a day every couple of months to have a range day so that you can clean up the place and make repairs to the targets and any other equipment that you have at the range.

Have a first aid kit available for minor cuts and make sure it has tweezers to pick out wood and steel sliver should you need it.

After you get a few events under your belt, you can look into putting on demonstrations for small groups like the Boy Scouts or at local sportsman shows in the area. Doing demonstrations are a great way to educate the public and to let them know that we are regular people and that we are serious about our sport and hobby.

Logo for the American Knife Throwers Alliance

The logo for the Knife, Axe, Tomahawk Throwing Association UK

PREPARING FOR A KNIFE- AND TOMAHAWK-THROWING COMPETITION

As the time for your first contest grows near, you will begin to have all sorts of things running through your head. Will I be good enough? Will I have the right knives? What do I do if I miss? First of all, knife and tomahawk people are some of the finest people you will ever meet. They come from all walks of life and most of the ones who travel the knife- and tomahawk-throwing circuit will do everything possible to make your first contest a great experience. I have seen older throwers give new throwers a set of knives to use in competition or to even take home if they did not bring the proper set that would be suitable for competition. I have seen knife throwers pull newbies aside and coach them to help them feel more comfortable.

In order to make your first event a memorable one, first take the time to do your homework. Find the website for the club and spend a few minutes familiarizing yourself with the rules from that club or organization. Find out what distances they throw from. Find out what size knife is acceptable. Find out what time they start and if they have a practice session beforehand. Check to see if lunch will be served or if refreshments are available. See if they have a score sheet that you can download and use for practice.

To prepare for the event, you need to make a plan for your training regimen. If you can find someone to throw knives with you, that will be a plus. You can use the sample score sheet if available. If one is not online, feel free to call or email the promoter and ask for one. They will be glad to help you and should be able to answer any other questions that you might have. Set aside some time every day to train. Try to include some physical conditioning and stretching exercises to ensure that you do not pull any muscles while in training. Go out either with your partner or alone and establish a baseline to see where your skills lie. From that first set of scores, you should be able to set some goals to improve where you are the weakest. If you are doing OK on the one spin, and not so good on the 1 ½ spin, spend a little extra time before you go through your normal routine to work on that 1½ spin throw to bring your score up.

Make a quick checklist of items to carry to the tournament.

1. Comfortable pair of shoes
2. Proper number of knives and tomahawks required to compete
3. Sheaths for knives and tomahawks
4. Clean rag to wipe down your knife to keep them dry
5. Oil or WD-40 for protection after you clean the knives and store them for the trip home
6. Towel for those humid days or to wipe the sweat from your hands in between throws
7. Water if not available at the site
8. Energy bars or snacks if not available at site
9. Insect repellant for outside events
10. Score sheet if available so you or your traveling companion can keep track of your score during competition

CHAPTER 5

HOW TO MAKE A
THROWING KNIFE

One of the questions that I get asked most often is how I make a throwing knife. Making a knife from scratch from your design and being able to throw it when you have completed it can be a very rewarding experience. I have been making knives professionally for thirty years, so I have a well-equipped shop. The average person who does not have access to the type of equipment that I have can still make a serviceable throwing knife with a minimum amount of tools and a lot of elbow grease.

In an attempt to simplify things, I am going to take you through the process on how I am able to make a throwing knife with a minimum amount of tools. I'll explain as I go, showing you how you can do the same with the tools that you may have available in your home shop or that you can purchase at the local home improvement store or hardware store. Even if you do not have the exact tools listed, you should be able to substitute certain tools for those that you have on hand. Since I do not know what equipment you have available, the following safety rules are pretty general and will serve as good safety rules for any knife shop.

SAFETY

All tools are dangerous if used improperly or carelessly. Working safely is the first thing the user or operator should learn because the safe way is the correct way. A person learning to operate machine tools must first learn the safety regulations and precautions for each tool or machine. Most accidents are caused by not following prescribed procedures. Develop safe work habits rather than suffer the consequences of an accident.

Most of the safety practices mentioned in this section are general in nature. Safety precautions for specific tools and machines should be available in the manuals that come with your particular tools or machines. Study these carefully and be on the alert to apply them.

EYE PROTECTION

Using eye protection in the machine shop is the most important safety rule of all. Metal chips and shavings can fly at great speeds and distances and cause serious eye injury. Safety glasses must be worn when working with handcutting tools, since most handcutting tools are made of hardened steel and can break or shatter when used improperly.

There are many different types of safety glasses available in the supply system; however, the ones that offer the best protection are the safety glasses with side shields. Safety goggles should be worn over prescription glasses.

HAZARDOUS NOISE PROTECTION

Noise hazards are very common in the machine shop. High intensity noise can cause permanent loss of hearing. Although noise hazards cannot always be eliminated, hearing loss is avoidable with earmuffs, earplugs, or both. These are generally available through the local hardware stores or the big box lumber stores.

The floor in a knife shop is often covered with razor-sharp metal chips, and heavy stock may be dropped on the feet. Therefore, safety shoes or a solid leather shoe must be worn at all times. Safety shoes are available in the supply system. These have a steel plate located over the toe and are designed to resist impact.

Tools

- Pair of scissors
- Permanent marker
- Piece of lightweight cardboard or a file folder
- Chop saw or angle grinder
- Hacksaw
- Flat file or bastard file
- Drill motor and a 3/16-inch bit
- Sturdy vise
- 120- , 220-, and 320-grit sandpaper

STEEL SELECTION

When making high quality throwing knives, I have always found that a spring steel such as 5160 or 1050 to be the best for the job. When heat-treated properly both steels will make an excellent throwing knife that will withstand the rigors of throwing for years to come. Such steel can be found at steel suppliers that specialize in steels for knifemakers. I will list the name of suppliers in the back of the book. The 1050 spring steel usually comes cold-rolled and available in annealed or tempered condition.

DESIGN

Even though throwing knives appear to be very basic in design, there are a few crucial elements that we want to incorporate into the design. My personal opinion is that you need at least three of the following qualities for a first-rate, professional grade throwing knife.

1. **Weight** for penetration
2. **Center-balanced** for throwing the knife by the blade or by the handle
3. **Length** for control
4. **The McEvoy formula**—1 ounce to 1¼ ounces of weight for every inch in length

I also like to design a throwing knife with a handle that is fairly straight with no huge curves or a bird's beak pommel that will interfere with the release of the knife when it is leaving your hand. I also favor steel that is a minimum of 3/16 inches thick, 1½ inches to 2 inches at the widest point and a minimum of 12 inches in length.

When first designing a new model, I like to draw the design out on paper and then when I have the basic design almost finalized, I cut the design out with a pair of scissors and transfer the design to a thicker piece of cardboard. Once you transfer the design over to a piece of cardboard, cut it out and hold it in your hand. The thicker cardboard should give you a better feel of how the new design will feel in your hand. You can take a ruler and run it along the length to find the center and mark it in the middle with a pen. Take the cardboard and rest it on your index finger on the template that you just made, and see if it will balance there. You may have to move it a little one way or the other to get it to balance. If it balances a little either way, you are very close and you should have a workable design.

Lets get started

Once you have chosen a design, you can purchase the appropriate size steel and lay your template on top of the bar. If the bar has a little mill scale on it, it will be a dark color. If it is shiny from being precision ground you can apply a light coat of layout fluid to color the steel so that you can see your scribe line.

Lay your pattern on top of the bar and use your scribe to mark along the pattern to make a line on the steel to transfer the pattern to the steel bar.

If you are taking the economical route, you will now put your bar in your vise with the point up and using your hacksaw, begin to saw out your knife, staying as close to the line as possible to begin removing the steel outside of your pattern.

When you finish removing steel from both sides, remove the piece of steel from the vise and place it back in the vise, point down, and begin removing the steel for the rest of the blade.

After you have the basic shape sawed out, you can place the steel back in the vise, edge up, and use your angle grinder to remove the final amount of steel down to the scribe line without going past the line. When you have a profile that now looks like a knife, take the angle grinder and make sure all burrs have been sanded down and grind a very slight bevel around the perimeter of the knife blank. You may also grind your main bevels towards the tip leaving them a little thick before heat treating and drill any holes so that you can attach the scales should your design call for scales.

Heat Treat Formula

I normally would not want or expect you to be able to perform the heat treating operations on your first throwing knife, but I would like for you

---

to do some research on the subject and search for a knifemaker in your town who has the proper equipment and can possibly heat treat your blade for a small fee. If you can manage to acquire the equipment, you can use the chart below to reach the desired hardness that should allow you to build a quality throwing knife that will last for years.

Hard Temp   1500°F - 1550° F
Oil Quench   Rc 58
Temper at 600°F for 1 hours to achieve a Rockwell hardness of 45.

Final grinding and polishing

After you finish heat treating your blade, you will need to check it for straightness and warping. Assuming you have a straight blade with no warping you will need to take your knife and place it back in your vise to begin the final grind. Depending on what type of finish you want on your knife, you can rough grind it to the final thickness with the grinder that you used earlier. It is not necessary to polish it too much to end up with a decent throwing knife. You can do that later after you test it out on the range to make sure that it was heat treated properly.

Now that you have given it a thorough test out on the range, you can begin applying the final finish and fabricate and install the handles, if that is part of your design.

For this knife, we will take it down to a 320-grit finish which is sufficient for a throwing knife. Because hand finishing is very detailed work, I am going to give you a very brief course on applying the final finish.

Go down to your local hardware or big box home improvement store and get some 180-, 200-, and 320-grit sandpaper. I like using a little light oil or WD-40 when sanding out a blade.

Secure the blade point out towards you in your vise. For extra safety, wrap the point up about an inch from the tip with lots of masking tape or duct tape. **Be very careful when walking away or bending down to**

pick up something off the floor as the point can hurt you even when taped up.

If you have tools laying around, find an old flat file and then cut a few strips of the 180-grit sandpaper and wrap it around the file once or twice with the grit to the outside keeping it flat with the file. Apply a small amount of light oil or WD-40 to the blade and sand from the handle to the tip of the blade keeping the file straight and making nice smooth cuts from the handle to the tip over and over again until you begin to see the color of the heat-treated blade begin to disappear. Keep up this motion, changing the sandpaper when it appears to not be cutting properly until all of the heat treat color is gone. When you are comfortable that you have a nice even finish on your blade, repeat the process with the 200- and 320-grit sandpaper.

After you have a nice finish that you are satisfied with, carefully remove the tape that is around the tip and carefully sand the final inch of the tip using the same process.

When the tip and flat part of the blade are finished, you can once again wrap the tip with tape for safety. Now you can remove the blade from the vise and secure it once again vise, this time with the edge of the blade up.

Firmly secure the blade in the vise. If you rounded the corners of the blade before heat treating the blade you will need to finish the rounding of the edges of the blade to eliminate any sharp edges, giving the blade a good feeling when you are holding it in your hand. Cut some more strips of sandpaper and fold them over a few times and perform a shoe-shine motion back and forth to finish rounding the edges. Using this process, go from 180-, 200-, and 320-grit until you have nice rounded edges. Flip the blade over in the vise and repeat on the opposite side.

HANDLES

Over the years, I have only used three types of handle material for throwing knives. I have used leather, vulcanized fiber, and G-10.

Leather makes a great handle matter for a throwing knives and is widely used in muzzle loading contests where you are required to dress in period attire and all of your accoutrements must be made from materials that were used during that period.

Vulcanized fiber is a laminated plastic composed of only cellulose. The material is a tough, resilient material that is lighter than aluminum, tougher than leather, and stiffer than most thermoplastics.

G10 laminate grades are produced by inserting continuous glass-woven fabric impregnated with an epoxy resin binder while forming a sheet under high pressure. This material is used extensively in the electronics industry because its water absorption is extremely minimal and the G10 line of materials is not electrically conductive. The G10 is most commonly used in PCB (Printed Circuit Boards) applications. The G10 exhibits superior mechanical and dimensional stability and doesn't shrink. Temperature ratings of 180 degrees Celsius. In addition to these properties, G10 has excellent dielectric loss properties and great electrical strength. The G10 is also known as Micarta and Garolite and can be used for structural supports, buss bars, mechanical insulation, gears, test fixtures, washers, spacers, and tight tolerance machined parts for electromechanical assemblies.

Safety precautions must be observed when working any handle materials that produce dust and fine particles.

A Little Movie Magic

As a professional knife and tomahawk thrower, I have served as a consultant to many production companies who seek my knowledge when planning knife and tomahawk scenarios for their projects. Even with the use of modern technology such as blue or green screens where they are able to insert computer graphic images or CGI, on occasion, they have a use for a physical knife thrower to be on the set as a either a consultant or a working knife thrower to perform certain knife-throwing stunts for a particular scene to add the realism into their film. Back in 2004, I was contacted by a production company to be a part of a film starring Salma Hayek, Penelope Cruz, and Dwight Yoakam titled *Bandidas*.

I was hired to teach Salma Hayek to look like a knife thrower as well as to teach her how to throw knives. I was also asked to design and make all of the throwing knives that were to be used for the film. The knives would have to fit in that period in history that the movie was based upon.

I first flew to Los Angeles with the intent of training Hayek over a weekend. However, at her request, I was sent to location down in Mexico City to continue her training. I trained her while on set and acted as a consultant for the knife-throwing scenes.

I once again was asked to fly to Durango, Mexico, to work with the second-unit people. This consisted of the stunt people who would be filming some of the basic stunts, and I was to teach the stunt actor how to look like knife thrower and how to hold the knife, etc. Then for my part, I had to do the actual knife throwing with cameras on all side of me filming my arms and hands from various angles, and they would use Hollywood magic to insert the actress into the scene.

So I have a few photos to show how we performed some of the stunts where throwing the actual knife would not have been practical, as well as some of the photos from the set on location to give you an idea how films are made.

We had to climb a couple hundred feet up the mountain to get to the set

Salma Hayek throwing one of the bowie knives that I made for the film.

One of the multiple set of knives that were made by me for the film

One of my bowie knives being worn by an actor

The stunt double for Salma Hayek learning how to handle the pair of bowie knives under my direction

Here, they are filming the actress simply hurling the knives towards a makeshift target that I fabricated on set. They just wanted to film her throwing the knives and then they would use me to film the actual throw.

They wanted to throw my bowie knife at this empty chili can and they would film it tumbling over the log. Once I told them that the can was too light to be hit and impaled halfway through. I showed them how we could make it appear that it could be done. I impaled the knife in the can by holding the knife in one hand and the can in the other and pushed the knife through the can. I then tied a string to the can so that when they filmed the scene, they could pull on the string and make it appear that the thrown knife hit the can and made it tumble over the log. They then filmed me actually throwing the knife and hitting the can point first and they created the illusion that it was done all in one motion.

The author and actress Salma Hayek in between filming.

Stories from the Field

When Harry met Harry

As someone who has been in the knife-throwing world for over thirty years, I have witnessed a lot of knife-throwing history being made and gotten to know the type of people who are attracted to knife throwing. Knife throwers come from all walks of life. We have had stock brokers, physicians, surgeons, and teachers, etc., who love to throw knives to help relieve the stress from their jobs. Some of them actually do quite well. To most people who are unfamiliar with knife throwers, there is this mystique that surrounds our little sport and hobby. A lot of knife throwers tend to be loners before they find us because of some of the misconceptions surrounding our sport. Knife throwing is a great exercise for hand to eye coordination and it is a great stress reliever. There is also a little exercise component built in as you are always walking back and forth to your target. You never know who you might meet along the way. One of my favorite stories was told to me by my good friend, Stephen McEvoy, and involved his father, a fairly new entertainer who has done quite well for himself.

First, let me tell you a thing or two about my friend and Stephen's father, Harry McEvoy. Harry McEvoy, who we referred to as "Mac," was a very modest gentleman who worked in the paint industry and loved any type of activity such as muzzleloading, archery, and knife throwing. He loved those activities so much that he wrote numerous articles and books on knife throwing for the muzzleloading community and he even wrote a book on archery. Harry was a family man and very traditional in many ways. He was no nonsense and spoke his mind, but was always tactful. Harry built a nice side business supplying throwing knives and tomahawks to the various retailers and collectors in the industry. To supplement his regular job he spent a lot of time promoting the sport of knife throwing for many years. He had quite a reputation for his high quality throwing knives.

One day, a twenty-four-year-old entertainer named Harry Connick Jr. asked if he could come over to visit with Harry. Apparently, he read one of Harry's books on knife throwing and wanted to meet and visit with Harry. He told Harry he was a performer and had an upcoming concert scheduled in the Detroit, Michigan area.

He apparently did not realize how far he was from Grand Rapids when he called Harry to set up the visit as he said he would arrive at about 3:00 PM that day. At about 6:00 PM he arrived at the door with two other young men whom he identified as his stage manager and one of his security people. All three were about the same age. As Harry was about to sit down to dinner, he suggested that they go up the corner to Mr. Burger and get some dinner themselves. He told them where to find the restaurant and invited them to return to the house in about half an hour.

When they returned, Harry Jr. asked Harry to take a look at the throwing knives he brought along. Harry Jr. opened the trunk of the car and showed him several examples of what turned out to be inexpensive knives masquerading as throwing knives. Harry examined the knives and remarked that they were "mostly junk." He then invited the boys to examine some "real" throwing knives and displayed several Tru-Balance throwing knife models. They all then went out back to throw the "real" knives. Harry offered some basic throwing instruction and they all took turns throwing knives for an hour or more that evening.

Stephen had to leave during the throwing session, but Harry called Stephen later and advised that they purchase several hundred dollars worth of new Tru-Balance knives. Harry Jr. also graciously invited Harry to attend his concert as his guest, but Harry declined because of distance and other considerations. All in all, Stephen said it was a very enjoyable evening even though his father was not fully aware of the already established celebrity of Harry Connick, Jr.

Harry was a great man and treated everyone equally. To Harry, they were just fellow knife throwers who he could spend time with and educate. Over the years, Stephen and I still talk about the visit and we still get a chuckle about the day that Harry met Harry.

Looking for Mr. Whitecloud

After meeting Harry McEvoy in the early '80s, and purchasing his books that listed the who's who of the professional knife throwers, it soon became my passion to seek out my knife-throwing heroes. I managed to find some of the greats like Paul LaCross through a friend of mine, and Larry Cisewski who I tracked down after seeing him in *Blade* magazine. Larry later purchased knives from me and we soon became good friends. Larry also introduced me to Sylvester Braun who was a great showman and performed with his wife in an act that consisted of whips, ropes and knives. The knife thrower who intrigued me most was also the most elusive. Kenneth Pierce, who used the stage name Che Che Whitecloud, had seemed to vanish off of the face of the earth.

Sylvester Braun sent me a copy of a weekly periodical named the *Circus Report*. The *Circus Report* keep close tabs on every one who had any type of circus act—it was considered the bible for the industry. I quickly subscribed to the magazine and began calling anyone who I thought might be able to tell me how to get in touch with Che Che White Cloud. After many, many months, and much frustration I saw a notice for the Rolling Thunder Circus with Che Che that was going to be traveling through the Aiken, South Carolina on their way through Georgia. I called the number trying to find out the location where the circus was going to set up. After many calls they finally told me that the tour was not coming through that town.

Feeling disappointed once again, I managed to get a direct number for the Rolling Thunder circus to call. I finally got to speak with a lady who said that her name was Nancy and that she was Che Che's friend at the time. She told me that he had heard about me from Mr. McEvoy and would love to have me make some knives for him. She asked if we could meet them at the Rolling Thunder Circus as they made their way through South Carolina in the city of Spartanburg, South Carolina which would be their only stop in South Carolina. I was on cloud nine as I called my wife and told her what just happened. I asked her if she was up for the three hour ride the next day to meet Che Che and Nancy.

My wife, Brenda, said "Yes, let's go." She knew how long I had been waiting to meet them. I picked Brenda up early from work the following day and we embarked on our journey up state to finally meet the famous and elusive Che Che White Cloud. After a few missed turns, we saw the Armory where the Circus was set up. We carefully pulled in and parked, and then made our way to the entrance. As we were walking, I knew this was the spot because off to the side we saw a huge Dually pickup truck with a large travel trailer attached. On the front of the truck was a license plate with something to the effect of CHE CHE WHITECLOUD THE WORLD'S GREATEST KNIFE THROWER. I smiled at Brenda and took a picture.

As we approached the entrance I asked the lady at the ticket counter where I might be able to find Che Che and Nancy? She replied, "Hi, I'm Nancy and Che Che is inside setting up for the next show." We exchanged a few pleasantries and purchased our tickets and walked inside to find a seat. This was our first Circus and we had no idea what to expect. Brenda and I began to look over the area to see if we could spot Che Che, but wasn't able to find anyone. I walked over to grab us a snack and began speaking with the guy who was selling the hot dogs and lo and behold, it was Che Che. He explained that it was a small Circus and in between performances everyone had a job. From setting up, selling merchandise and food to cleaning up ahead of the next show, then breaking down to move to the next town. They would do two or three shows a day and then pack up and move to the next town and do it all over again.

Soon after this chance meeting, the Circus began with a variety of performers, while I kept my eyes open for Che Che. It was not long until I saw him sneak out of the vendor area to reappear in full Native American regalia as the spinning wheel of death was set into place. He was an impressive figure and I hoped it demonstrated to Brenda why I had searched so long and hard to find him. He began his number by walking out in his attire and spinning a knife in the palm of his hand like a top as his assistant took her place against the wheel. Next Che Che got into position and began firing off knife and after knife in rapid succession, landing them within inches of his assistant's body. His first trick was received with thunderous applause. Brenda and I sat on the edge of our seats, as the assistant would stand in different poses while Che Che outlined her with knives. Then for the finale, Che Che would strap his assistant to the Wheel of Death and quickly spin the wheel. Once he was in position he fired off nine knives in a matter of seconds and then ran up to stop the wheel and release his assistant. This final act received another amazed round of applause from the audience. As quickly as he had come out he was gone, I managed to catch a glimpse of him walking back to the vendor area as the crowds began to disperse.

Brenda and I just sat back enjoying what we just witnessed as the crowds moved out and then we walked over to finally meet Che Che and Nancy and to spend a little time with them before the next per-formances that evening. During our talks, Che Che mentioned that he had heard good things about me from Harry McEvoy and wanted me to make him a set of knives. We talked a little more and exchanged phone numbers so that we could stay in touch. It was a day that Brenda and I will always remember and cherish to this day. Che Che and Nancy have visited us many times over the years and they are still among our closest friends and I am still a huge fan of Che Che White Cloud, the greatest knife thrower in the world.

IN CLOSING

I can only hope that I have achieved what I set out to do when writing this book. I tried to give the reader an all-inclusive look at the world of knife throwing from the early pioneer's to the modern day knife and tomahawk thrower. I tried to simplify the parts on how to throw a knife and how to make a knife so that it was easy to understand for anyone at any level. I wanted to touch briefly on no-spin knife throwing as it has become very popular over the last decade. It is a little more instinctive style of throwing and requires a lot of practical experience on the range to become proficient. I wanted you to get a good taste of what is involved so that you can experiment on your own. My good friend, Ralph Thorn, has an excellent DVD on the no-spin style where you can continue your studies where I left off. Thank you for your support and I hope that this book will serve you well throughout your journey in the world of knife and tomahawk throwing. As they say, it is not about the destination, it is all about the journey. I am happy to be able to play a small part in your journey.

—Bobby Branton

Links and Information

Throwing Knife and Tomahawk suppliers

Tru Balance Knife Company EAST

PO Box 807

Awendaw, SC 29429

843-928-3624

www.tru-balanceknives-east.com

Branton Knife Company

PO Box 807

Awendaw, SC 29429

843-928-3624

www.brantonknives.com

Tru-Balance Knife Company

PO Box 140555

Grand Rapids, MI 49514

616-647-1215

Bill Page
PO Box 3312
Montgomery, AL. 36109

Joseph Darrah
1126 Edgewood Ave.
Berwyn, PA 19312

Kings Forge and Tomahawks
156 Rattlesnake Hill
Cleveland GA 30528
706-969-3027
www.kingsforgeandmuzzleloading.com

Cold Steel
Cold Steel, Inc.
6060 Nicolle Street
Ventura, CA 93003
800-255-4716
Fax: 805-642-9727
www.coldsteel.com

Beaver Bill
513-756-1983
www.beaverbill.com

H&B Forge
235 Geisinger Road
Shiloh, OH 44878
419-895-1856
www.hbforge.com

RMJ Tactical
866.779.6922 / 423.756.4300

www.rmjtactical.com

Flying Steel
484-474-0304

www.flyingsteel.com

KNIFEMAKING SUPPLIERS

Pop's Knives and Supplies
103 Oak Street

Washington, GA 30673

706-678-5408

www.popsknifesupplies.com

Sheffields Knifemakers Supply
1-800-874-7007

www.sheffieldsupply.com

New Jersey Steel Baron
973-949-4140

newjerseysteelbaron.com

Paragon Heat Treat Ovens
Paragon Industries, L.P.,

2011 South Town East Blvd.

Mesquite, Texas 75149-1122

1-800-876-4328

www.paragonweb.com/Heat_Treating_Furnaces.cfm

Admiral Steel
4152 West 123rd Street

Alsip, IL 60803

708-388-9600

800-323-7055

www.admiralsteel.com

Midwest Knifemakers supply LLC
1350 Lake Street

North Mankato, MN 56003

507-720-6063

www.usaknifemaker.com

Alpha Knife Supply
425-868-5880

www.alphaknifesupply.com

Riverside Machine
870-642-7643

www.riversidemachine.net

Knifekits.com
877-255-6433

www.knifekits.com

Jantz Supply
309 W Main

Davis, OK 73030

800-351-8900

www.knifemaking.com

Texas Knifemakers Supply
10649 Haddington # 180
Houston, TX 77043
888-461-8632
www.texasknife.com

Evenheat Heat Treat Ovens
PO Box 399
6949 Legion Road
Caseville, Michigan 48725
989-856-2281
www.evenheat-kiln.com

Knife Throwing Organizations and Resources

www.AKTA-USA.com

www.eurothrowers.org

www.knifethrowing.info

www.ikthof.com

THROWING KNIFE
COMPANIES

Tru-Balance Knife Company EAST

www.tru-balanceknives-east.com

Branton Knife Company

www.brantonknives.com

Tru-Balance Knife Company

PO Box 140555

Grand Rapids, MI 49514-0555

616-647-1215

INDEX

ALSO AVAILABLE

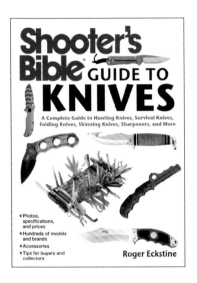

Shooter's Bible Guide to Knives
A Complete Guide to Hunting Knives, Survival Knives, Folding
Knives, Skinning Knives, Sharpeners, and More
by Roger Eckstine

The new *Shooter's Bible Guide to Knives* sets the standard for comprehensive publications by carrying on the Shooter's Bible tradition of bringing together more products and information than any other source. With photographs and descriptions of more than 400 knives, readers are treated to product highlights from major manufacturers and custom knife makers. This book brings you from the blacksmith shop to high tech influential designers with insights into blade steel, locking mechanisms, and handle materials. When it comes to knives, this book is the source for the products and the passion.

$19.95 Paperback • ISBN 978-1-61608-577-3

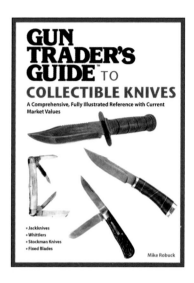